bc10161325

THE
PERPETUAL
MIRACLE

with faith in the future
of

FAIRMOUNT CHURCH

Frank Ferris

THE
PERPETUAL MIRACLE

STUDIES IN THE TEACHING OF JESUS

by

FRANK HALLIDAY FERRIS

THE BOBBS-MERRILL COMPANY, INC.
Publishers

INDIANAPOLIS   NEW YORK

FIRST EDITION

The Library of Congress has cataloged this publication as follows:

Ferris, Frank Halliday. The perpetual miracle; studies in the teaching of
Jesus. [1st ed.] Indianapolis, Bobbs-Merrill [1959] 191 p. 19 cm. 1. Jesus
Christ—Teachings. I. Title. BS2415.F4 232.9 59–9847 ‡ Library of
Congress

TO MINNA PROCTOR FERRIS

SOCIAE BONAE RERVM HVMANARVM
DIVINARVMQVE

TABLE OF CONTENTS

Follow Me

The Way, the Truth and the Life

O Thou who in thy Son hast shown us
   the way for feet that stumble,
   the truth for minds perplexed,
   the life for hearts that fail and break,
   help us to follow him so truly
   that we may learn of him
   the secret of his strength and peace and joy.
So may his grace abide with us always. Amen.

FOLLOW ME

Jesus did not ask to be worshiped. He asked to be followed. "Follow me": this often repeated imperative presents his religion in congenial terms, in terms not of creed but of action. The Jesus we find most appealing is the Jesus of action who, when he saw someone in trouble or an evil which needed redress, did something about it, not next day or next week, but then and there.

It was this trait, not his preaching, which cost him his life, for it was his cleansing of the temple that sealed his fate. Had he merely talked about the money changers perhaps nothing would have happened. But he did something—overturned their tables and drove them out. It was more than the Sadducees, the temple authorities who got a cut on the concession, could take.

Matthew, the best known gospel because it stands first in the New Testament, presents Jesus as teacher. But Mark, the earliest gospel, based on the memories of Peter, portrays him as a man of action, a virile, forceful, decisive figure. It is hard to see how he crowded so much into the few swift months of his ministry. His strenuous life is the more astounding because it was lived not in an energetic climate like ours among energetic people but in an enervating, subtropical climate in the languorous, slow-moving Near East. Luke summarizes it in the tenth chapter of Acts: "He went about doing good."

Luke tells us also that while outsiders called the early followers of Jesus Christians, the Christians themselves spoke of their religion—in terms of motion—as "the Way" and of themselves as "those of the Way." This metaphor of the way runs all through the New Testament. "I must go on my way." "Narrow is the way that leads to life." "The new and living way which he opened for us." In the fourteenth chapter of John is the brief allegory of the way. "You know the way where I am going," says Jesus. Thomas objects: "Lord, we do not know where you are going. How can we know the way?" Jesus answers, "I am the way"—you cannot see the end of the road, you cannot reach it in a step, but keep on following me.

We often wonder whether we have a right to call ourselves Christian—our lives are so obviously subChristian. Yes, we have the right if we define a Christian as I used to define him to my communicant class: a Christian is one who keeps on following Jesus, who, when he stumbles and falls, picks himself up and tries again.

Can We Follow Him?

It is interesting to run down with a concordance the number of times Jesus said, "Follow me," to whom and under what circumstances he said it. But a prior query for many

thoughtful folk is, Can we follow him? The question Francis
Palgrave asked a century ago is even more pressing now:

> Dim tracts of time divide
>   Those golden days from me,
> Thy voice comes strange
>   O'er years of change:
> How can I follow thee?
>
> Comes faint and far thy voice
>   From vales of Galilee,
> The vision fades
>   In ancient shades:
> How could we follow thee?

Some say it is impossible to follow him because we don't
know enough about him. Dean Inge says that the attempt
to write a life of Jesus should be given up; the material for it
does not exist. Anderson Scott in his article on Jesus in the
Encyclopaedia Britannica says the same. Santayana in *The
Idea of Christ in the Gospels* describes Jesus as a legendary
figure so buried beneath the accretions of legend that it is impossible to recover him. Those who hold this view feel that
not only is the gospel record meager but also that what we
have is not history but interpretation, a reflection not so
much of what Jesus himself said and did as what early Christians believed about him, what the early church taught
about him.

There is some truth in this. The first three gospels—the
synoptics we call them, meaning "having the same point of

view"—are photographs but not identical photographs. They are taken from different angles. In Matthew and Luke the negatives have been retouched: in Matthew (the Jewish gospel), to make Jesus appear as the fulfillment of Messianic prophecy, conforming to the pictures of the Messiah in Jewish prophecy and apocalypse—not an easy thing to do; in Luke (the gentile gospel), to present Jesus not as the Messiah of the Jews but as the Saviour of the world. Mark (the martyr gospel, the Roman gospel) is highly regarded today because it is the earliest, the simplest, the one that comes closest to the human Jesus. But even scholars who accept the tradition that Peter's witness is behind it think it may reflect the ideas and practices of the church in Rome about the year 70. The Fourth Gospel is not a photograph but a portrait of Jesus as seen through the eyes of a mystic—the greatest of mystics— who is interested not so much in the Jesus who lived once in Palestine as in the Jesus who lives always in those who love him.

Others hold that, while we do not have all the information we want about Jesus, we have all we need. Says Professor J. Hardy Ropes of Harvard, "There is nothing that needs to be known about Jesus that cannot be had by anyone who will read Mark with open eyes." Says another eminent New Testament scholar, Dr. Ernest De Witt Burton, the University of Chicago, "If the main facts in the life of Jesus are not historically trustworthy, nothing is."

The gospels are not objective history. They are propaganda, an appeal from faith to faith. What John says of his gospel is equally true of the earlier three: "These things are written that you may believe that Jesus is the Christ, the Son of God, and believing may have life in his name." But after turning the pages of the gospels for many years, I offer to you my judgment that the men who wrote them were reliable reporters who, while not infallible, while each has his special interest and emphasis, yet give us a picture of Jesus which is consistent and clear. No one can read them without discovering what kind of man he was and what were the ruling ideas of his mind. Do we know enough about Jesus to follow him? My answer is yes.

But what we have is a map, not a blue print. In 1896 a Topeka minister, Dr. Charles M. Sheldon, wrote a novel called *In His Steps*. Of all our American best sellers, it was *the* best seller: its sale ran into the millions. Its hero regulated his conduct by one simple and appealing test, What would Jesus do?

The plain fact is that in many of today's tangled situations we do not know what he would do. How would he stand as between management and labor in industrial disputes? between the free enterprise system and the welfare state? What would be his attitude toward power diplomacy, "negotiation from strength," as Secretary Dulles calls it? toward the implacable feud between the Arabs and his own people, the Jews? toward the aspirations of Communist Russia and Communist China? toward amusements such as cocktail parties and gambling games? toward dividends, money obtained without earning it? toward the shifting conception of sex relationships? Jesus does not relieve his followers of the responsibilities of moral freedom. We have to think out these problems ourselves. We do know the principles by which he lived and which he commended to his followers.

Is His Teaching Too Hard to Follow?

Some say we cannot follow him because his principles are too high.

> How very hard it is to be
> A Christian! hard for you and me . . .
> To realize it more or less
> With even the moderate success
> Which commonly repays our strife
> To carry out the aims of life.

So wrote Browning a century ago in words which anticipate our present plight.

Dr. Harry Emerson Fosdick in his autobiography, *The Living of These Days,* makes it plain that the burning question in his early life, the question with which he had to wrestle, was, Is Christianity credible? Can we believe its story of a god-man or man-god who lived and died and rose again? Today the burning question is, Is Christianity practical? Will it work in a world like ours?

The Fourth Gospel reports that on one occasion his disciples said to Jesus, "This is a hard saying. Who can listen to it?" Many of his sayings are hard sayings still—not hard to understand, hard to follow. Mark Twain said that his difficulty with the Christian religion was not with the parts he couldn't understand but with the parts he could.

Here are a few samples from Matthew's masterly compilation of Jesus' ethical teaching which we know as The Sermon on the Mount:

> You have heard that it was said to the men of old, "You shall not kill. Whoever kills shall be liable to judgment." But I say to you that everyone who is angry with his brother shall be liable to judgment.
>
> You have heard that it was said, "You shall not commit adultery." But I say to you that everyone who looks at a woman lustfully has already committed adultery with her in his heart. If your right eye causes you to sin, pluck it out and throw it away; better to lose one of your members than that your whole body be thrown into hell. If your right hand causes you to sin, cut it off and throw it away; better to lose one of your members than that your whole body go to hell.
>
> You have heard that it was said, "An eye for an eye and a tooth for a tooth." But I say to you, Do not resist one who is evil. But if anyone strikes you on the right cheek, turn to him the other also. If anyone takes your coat, let him have your cloak as well. If anyone forces you to go one mile, go with him two miles. Give to him who begs from you, and do not refuse him who would borrow.
>
> You have heard that it was said, "You shall love your neighbor and hate your enemy." But I say to you, Love your enemies and pray for those who persecute you, so that you may be sons of your Father who is in heaven; for he makes his sun rise on the evil and on the good, he sends rain on the just and the unjust.

Then comes the summary, the key sentence of The Sermon

on the Mount, the key sentence in the ethical teaching of
Jesus: "You therefore must be perfect as your heavenly Father
is perfect."

Are such teachings practical in a world like this? Can we
follow them? What nation has ever made non-violence, non-
reprisal, non-resistance to evildoers the cornerstone of its
foreign policy? What would happen to one that did? What
are you going to do when a mad man like Hitler runs amuck?
The only world figure of our time who consistently followed
this policy was Gandhi, who was not a Christian but a Hindu,
though influenced by Jesus via Tolstoi.

Come down to the individual. Do you find it easy to love
your enemies, to reproduce the impartial, undiscourageable,
magnanimous good will which Jesus attributes to God? How
do you feel toward unfriendly folk, the people who snub you,
lie about you, cheat you, take advantage of you? When someone does me an injury, I have no inclination to retaliate. My
inclination is to avoid him from then on. But Jesus does not
say, "Avoid your enemies." He says, "Love your enemies.
Try to change them into friends."

Phillips Brooks used to tell seminary students that no
preacher ought to set before his people ideals he did not intend
and expect them to realize. Did Jesus err in pitching his teaching so high?

A Flying Goal

The first thing to be said is that no responsible teacher can
present the way of Jesus as an easy vocation. Always its appeal has been to the moral athlete, the man who is willing to

discipline his mind and spirit as the men who run a mile in four minutes discipline their bodies. For most of us some of the time, for some all the time, the way of self-indulgence is more attractive than the way of self-discipline.

The second thing to be said is that, hard as the Christian way is, there is no satisfying alternate to it. Try to name one. Secularism, the organization of life apart from God? Materialism, the worship of things which either leave us or we leave them? Communism with its atheism and totalitarianism? Stoicism, the resolution to grit your teeth and brave life through with what Bertrand Russell calls "unyielding despair"? The more we consider it, the more we are driven to Peter's conclusion. When Jesus' fair-weather followers were deserting him in droves, he asked his disciples, "Will you also go away?" Peter answered, "To whom shall we go?"*

The third thing to be said is that to the Christian athlete there is something exhilarating about a flying goal, the everfailing, never-ceasing quest of perfection. It is the secret of continual progress. If we had an easy goal, a stationary goal, we could reach it, then stop. With an absolute standard before us, we need never stop. We shall never reach it in this life, but the New Testament encourages us to think that our horizon is not bounded by this life.

The fourth thing to be said is that the Christian religion is based not on what we can do for ourselves but on what God can do for us. This is the heart of Paul's gospel: we are saved by grace through faith (Ephesians 2:8) even though we must

---

* For a fuller consideration of this episode, see the last chapter.

work out our own salvation (Philippians 2:12). The reason we can work out our own salvation is that God is at work in us (Philippians 2:13). We are saved not by what we do for God but by what he does for us. Our part is simply to accept his offer—the response of faith to the offer of grace. It is not where we are at a given moment which determines our destiny but the direction in which we are facing, the goal toward which we are striving. We are in the way and on the way as long as we can say with Paul, "I count not myself yet to have laid hold, but I press on" (Philippians 3:13, 14).

Jesus called his followers disciples. Disciple, as everyone knows, means learner. "Learn of me," he said. One test of our discipleship is our willingness to keep being educated by him. But anyone who has tried to become educated in any field knows that you never come to the end of it, never know all there is to be known, because in every field the boundaries are constantly being extended. This is conspicuously true in the physical sciences such as physics and astronomy, and it is true even of so fixed (you might suppose) a subject as the Bible. Even had I learned all that was known in my seminary days, I should still have much to learn because of the new knowledge which is constantly coming through philology—the mastery of languages not previously known—and through archaeology—the Dead Sea scrolls are the most dramatic discovery but there have been others as important. I still have a long road ahead of me, but I am farther on my way than when I began.

You know how in school we keep coming back to the same subject but on a higher level. The student approaches United States history three times, first in elementary school, again in

junior high, again in senior high—each time more fully. Then
if he wants to go into it he can study it in college and graduate
school. In the church school the life of Jesus is studied three
times, each time on a more mature level. So it is with following Jesus. We never come to the end of the road but we
progress along it. Luther said that a man never is a Christian
but always becoming one.

Last summer I stood beside Profile Lake and looked up at
the Old Man of the Mountain. Of course I thought of Hawthorne's "The Great Stone Face." A boy lived in the presence of that benignant image so admiringly and devotedly
that gradually he came to resemble it. One day the neighbors
looked at him in astonishment and said, "Ernest himself is the
Great Stone Face." We Christians live in the presence of an
unattainable ideal. But if we steadily expose ourselves to it we
find that through the years it has been working in us and
through us, that we are closer to it than when we began.

Learning by Doing

One of modern pedagogy's most seminal ideas is learning
by doing. It is not new. Galileo is called the father of the ex-
perimental method. Long before Galileo a Roman sage said,
"*Discimus ambulando*"—we learn by walking, we learn as
we walk. It has been revived in our time. The emphasis is on
learning not by rote but by expressional activity. Busy work
it is called in kindergarten; at a more advanced stage, the
project method or the laboratory method; at a still higher level,
research. Even in language study the trend is away from the

old system of paradigms of declensions and conjugations, toward the inductive or conversational approach. As one speaks a language, gets the taste of it in his mouth, the sound of it in his ear, unconsciously its inflections and idioms fall into place. None of the arts and crafts can be learned save by practice, but as a man works at it he gradually perceives the principles which underlie it. "If any man wills to do God's will, he shall know of the teaching," the Fourth Gospel reports Jesus to have said. That is the project method applied to religion.

As we brood over unsolved mysteries we wonder, Why did not Jesus make this plain? We forget that there are two kinds of teachers. One is interested in learning for its own sake. The other is interested in learning in order to do something, to become something. Jesus was the second kind. He was a carpenter—not a philosopher but a craftsman.

You cannot learn carpentry from a book any more than you can learn to swim from a book. You have to get the feel of the tools in your hand. The only way to hit a nail on the head is to act as though you could, then try. Jesus says to act as though you are a child of God, as though the people around you are too, as though they are going to work with you rather than against you. In temptation act as though with God's help you are going to win. As you work at the Christian craft, much that was once mysterious becomes plain.

The Christian is a learner, then a follower. It is a logical sequence. When a man learns a trade or a profession, it is natural to suppose he intends to follow it. Is anything more futile than learning for learning's sake? A man doesn't become a scholar merely by sitting in a library, absorbing the contents of books. He must be constantly giving out—lecturing, writing, teaching—if he wants to increase his own capacity to learn.

One reason the man in the street is not impressed by college diplomas, Phi Beta Kappa keys, Doctor of Philosophy degrees and other insignia of learning is that they do not always indicate the ability to translate knowledge into action, fine theories into fine deeds. "By their fruits you will know them," said Jesus, not by what they say or what they know, but by what they do. What a sound ideal was that of the fourteenth century mystic: "I would fain be to the Eternal Goodness what a man's hand is to a man." The hand is the organ by which a man translates knowledge into action.

The Test of Obedience

Someone has said that there are three ways of finding Christ: the way of love, the way of faith, the way of obedience. Some respond to the beauty of Jesus' life. Said Clement of Alexandria, true Greek that he was, "He is so lovely as to be alone loved by us whose hearts are set on the true beauty." There are those today who fall in love with him who is altogether lovely and infinitely fair, and loving him come to believe in and follow him. Others find him by the way of faith. They believe in him, then come to love and follow him. But most of us find him by the way of obedience. We start to follow him and as we follow come to love and trust him.

"Follow me": it is the crucial test. In the *Alumni Bulletin* of Union Theological Seminary, President Henry P. Van Dusen quotes a letter from a young minister:

> I am weary of the endless stream of books on all levels of profundity which call on Christians to contemplate their own navels. As a pastor I am aware of my people's problems, anxieties, tensions. They need to understand themselves. But most of all they need a Master to follow, a cause to give themselves to. Jesus' call, "Follow me," is still the most authentic note in the New Testament. When we get our people to take that call seriously, we shall be on our way to a healthier, more vital Christian faith. Undoubtedly the twelve disciples had inner conflicts and personality quirks, but Jesus focused their attention outward—and this is our chief concern as ministers today.

"To that diagnosis and that prescrpition," says Dr. Van Dusen, "I respond with a fervent Amen."

"Follow me." This was the only test our Lord imposed on his first disciples. In the first chapter of John he says it to Philip. In the last chapter he says it to Peter. In the tenth chapter, in the Parable of the Sheepfold, he says, "My sheep hear my voice and follow me; and I give them eternal life, and no one shall snatch them out of my hand."

"Follow me." In the fourth chapter of Matthew he says it to four sturdy fishermen. Straightway they left their nets and followed. In the ninth chapter he says it to a tax collector at work in his office. He saw the lights and shadows play across the man's face, the darkness of a moral struggle, then the

calm of a deep peace. "Follow me," he said. Matthew left
his office and followed.

Notice that he called men from their work. Not one of
his disciples belonged to the leisure class. If you want something done, go to a man who is already doing something, who
feels at home in his working clothes. So Jesus thought when
he chose his first followers. He never hid from them what
following involved. We read that he said to them, "If any
man would come after me, let him deny himself and take up
his cross and follow me."

Some could not meet the test. A young man comes to Jesus.
He is well to do, well born, well bred. He tells Jesus he has
kept all the commandments, asks what he lacks. Jesus bids
him "sell what you have and give to the poor and follow me."
The young man turns sorrowfully away. There are thousands
of his type. They are attracted to Jesus. They have an amiable wish that his cause may succeed. They come to church
when the weather is not too bad or too good. They drop an
offering in the plate. But when it comes to following where
he leads, they draw back. Well-mannered, well-disposed,
mildly pious people—willing to follow a little way, but not
all the way.

Jesus would never accept such half-hearted allegiance. A
would-be disciple says, "Lord, let me first go bury my father."
Jesus answers, "Follow me. Leave the dead to bury their own
dead." It sounds harsh. The Chinese with their veneration
for their ancestors think it immoral—it has to be translated
very freely before it is acceptable to them. But Jesus does not
want a follower who lets anything turn him aside. He wants

stout hearts who will follow where he leads and follow all the way.

What It Boils Down To

This is what the Christian religion boils down to, this is what it is all about: Can we follow him? Will we?

Not long ago a friend and I toured the Civil War battle-fields, tracing the course of the contending armies from Manassas to Appomattox. I supposed that the climax would be Gettysburg—that classic encounter, one of the decisive battles of history, the invasion of northern territory which was Lee's last bid for victory. When it failed, though the war dragged on for almost two years, the Confederacy was a lost cause. I was not disappointed in Gettysburg, but the place that had the most emotional content for me was Appomattox where Lee's ragged, hungry, weary men gave up their battle flags and stacked their arms in surrender.

As every school boy knows, the Civil War was fought by the North to preserve the union and free the slaves. With all its lamentable consequences, it accomplished those two ends. I have never been able to follow Lee's reasoning when after agonized soul searching he resigned his commission in the United States Army and cast his lot with the Confederacy. He was opposed to the war, opposed to secession, opposed to slavery. I can only think that—like most of us when it comes to extremes—he was swayed by sentiment, by ties of blood.

But Lee was a leader whom men could love, trust and

follow. The twenty-eight thousand who surrendered at Appomatox followed him to the end. The half-hearts had gone. During the ten-month siege of Petersburg while Grant was drawing the noose around the doomed city, they deserted by hundreds, by thousands. After Grant finally breached Lee's line and Lee began his last desperate retreat, the desertions continued. They may have thought the best thing to do was escape while they had a chance, get back to their homes and families. Who can blame them? Not I; I have little enough reason to suppose that I am cast in heroic mold. But twenty-eight thousand, the hard core of the Army of Northern Virginia, closed ranks and marched, marched, marched without rations and without rest until, with Meade pressing them from three sides and Sheridan's cavalry cutting off their retreat, there was nothing left but surrender. Those twenty-eight thousand were the heroes who followed their knightly leader all the way.

We Christians follow a Leader whose cause often looks like a forlorn hope. We see the half-hearts drop out when the going gets hard. Sometimes we are tempted to drop out. But always there are those who keep on. Said a great Christian of our own time, "Again and again I have been tempted to give up the struggle, but always that strange man on the cross sends me back to my task again." Always there are those who are able to say, "I have fought the good fight, I have finished the course, I have kept the faith."

So may it be with us who in this terrific generation are privileged to be his followers that we, coming to the end of the hard-fought day weary and spent but undishonored and un-dismayed, may look into our Leader's eyes and say, "We came with feet that faltered, but we came."

Lord Jesus, this commitment of which we have been think-ing must be made, not in groups, but one by one. Unworthy disciples have we been, following afar with halting steps and slow. Now give us what it takes to follow hard after thee, to press on toward the goal; for in all our best hours we want to follow thee. Amen.

The Dangers of Living

In Quietness and Confidence

The day returns and we return to thee,
    invoking thy benedictions on all that the day may bring.
We know not what the day may bring, but we know
    what kind of man can meet whatever the day brings.

Father, into thy hands we commit our spirits;
    into thy hands we commit those we love both near and
        far away;
    into thy hands we commit all whom this day finds in
        special need of thee,
    serene and sure that thou meanest nought but good to
        thy children;
    that in quietness and confidence shall be our strength,
    that as our days so shall our strength be,
    that in the midst of life's tumult thou wilt keep him in
        perfect peace whose mind is stayed on thee.

In this faith we resolve to live today
    quietly, calmly, hopefully, cheerfully, strongly.
May he who is full of grace and truth impress his
    character on ours. Amen.

THE DANGERS OF LIVING

SHORTLY BEFORE Robert Louis Stevenson's death on one of the Samoa Islands, a missionary wrote that he would like to come to talk to him "as to one in danger of dying." Stevenson answered that he did not want to talk about the danger of dying but would be glad to see him if he would talk about the dangers of living.

There is a sense in which Thoreau's dictum, "One world at a time," is wise. True, the Christian horizon is not restricted to this world. According to the New Testament, the consequence of sin is not confined to this world. There is a moral continuity between this world and the next; the character we carry out of this world is the character we carry into the next. And, because our character is our fate, reward and punishment are automatic.

Jesus consistently speaks of this life as being of decisive moral significance, as though here the soul acquires a mold, a set, which is permanent. There is a finality in his words which every sensitive mind must feel, as in the sobering conclusion of his description of the Judgment: "These will go into eternal punishment, but the righteous into eternal life." Nevertheless, if we can overcome the dangers of living, we need not fear the danger of dying.

31

What are the dangers of living? Does Jesus, our chief expert in the art of living, throw any light upon them, point out any risks? Yes, there are five kinds of people whom he warns.

The People Who Are Hard

The first are those who are hard. It is these he has in mind in his description of the Judgment. Those on the right are astonished to find themselves there. "What have we done to be numbered among the blessed?" The King answers, "I was hungry and you gave me food, naked and you clothed me," and so on. They are unconvinced, think it a case of mistaken identity. "When did we see you hungry and feed you?" They do not remember because they are instinctively and habitually kind: we do not remember what we instinctively and habitually do. Wordsworth speaks of the "little, nameless, unremembered acts of kindness and of love" which are "the best portion of a good man's life." The acts are forgotten because they were second nature, the overflow of a heart of good will.

With those on the left it was the other way. They were not conscious of neglect. That was their condemnation. They were instinctively and habitually hard, insensitive to human need. Such Jesus warns. "I was hungry and you did not feed me." So familiar are the words that we are likely to limit them to their literal meaning. Do they not include deeper need than bread?

In the late forties the church I served took responsibility for bringing seventy displaced families from Europe and settling them in Cleveland—people of whom we knew nothing except that they were homeless and destitute and had been screened for contagious diseases. I can speak of it for I had no part in it; it was done by a large and capable committee. They found homes for these families when housing was tight. They found jobs for the breadwinners with employers who were willing to take them sight unseen. In the undercroft of the church was enough clothing to stock a clothing store, enough household goods to start a furniture store. Teams worked in shifts around the clock to clean, paint and furnish the dwellings, stock them with food and other necessities. Members of the committee met the families as they arrived, took them to homes ready to live in, escorted the breadwinners to their jobs. Fairmount Church won unsought recognition for the competence with which it carried through this project. On a smaller scale, it was repeated the country over.

Recently I "filled in" at a pastorless church in a grubby little town. The congregation numbered about a hundred, a fourth of whom were children from a nearby orphanage. On the One Great Day of Sharing, they put over four hundred dollars on the offering plates for overseas relief. When I asked an elder how they did it, he said, "We save up for it." When you lament this terrible time—man's inhumanity to man and all the rest—remember this on the other side: never has there been such a continuous outpouring for people we have never seen. When men need food, clothing, shelter, we do not fail. But man's deepest hunger is for friendship. Do we withhold it from those who need it? In the most lyric passage he ever wrote, Paul says, "If I bestow all my goods to feed the poor but have not love, it profits nothing."

In that day of perfect lucidity we call the Judgment, when the secrets of all hearts are revealed, will there be someone—perhaps one who for years was close to us in our home, our school, our office—who can say, "I was hungry for friendship and you did not give it to me"? If so, we come under the first class Jesus warned—the people who are hard.

Those Whose Thoughts Are Evil

The second class consists of those (you will find them described in Matthew 5:21-29) who do no actual wrong but cherish in imagination the delights they might have if they did what discretion or timidity keeps them from doing. They do not commit murder but they harbor cruel and vengeful thoughts; they picture to themselves what they'd like to do to the man they have it in for and gloat over real or imaginary misfortunes that befall him. They do not commit adultery but allow lustful thoughts to run unchecked through their minds and dally with wanton ideas until in imagination they experience what the roué experiences in fact. They know the meaning of Oscar Wilde's perverse epigram, "An improper mind is a continual feast."

When Kipling published *The Light that Failed*, Sir J. M. Barrie, then a young journalist, made this penetrating comment on its hero: "He thinks because he has knocked around the world in shady company he has nothing left to learn. It never dawns on him that he is a babe in arms compared with many men who have stayed at home with their mothers."

Character has been defined as what a man is in the dark. His inner life may be ugly while outwardly all is sweetness and light. Jesus insists that interior cleanliness is what counts. It is not the dirt that gets on a man's hand or goes into his mouth that defiles him, but the dirt that comes from within. "For from within come evil thoughts, murder, adultery, fornication, theft, slander. These are what defile a man."

Paul, with his deep psychology of sin, pushing it back (as Jesus does) from overt act to inner degradation, suggests that one form God's judgment may take is giving a man up to his own reprobate mind. As a burnt hand loses the sense of touch, as a dirty windshield makes the whole world look dirty even on a bright day, Paul says that the mind becomes darkened, stained, seared, so that it can no longer do what it was made to do—see and report truly.

You see a stone in the woods, writes John Burroughs. It looks clean, but turn it over and what a swarm of crawling things scamper to cover, shunning the light! "Whatever the color of your habitual thoughts," says Marcus Aurelius, "that color will your mind take, for the mind is dyed by its thoughts."

Indeed, the main effect of an unclean mind, a polluted imagination, is an ingrained coarsening of nature. Our faces, our conversations and the kinds of reading and entertainment we prefer all give evidence of it. We have an emotional leaning to the good, the beautiful, the true; but habitual wrong thinking predisposes us to the vulgar and the vile. Thus we make our own hell.

Evil thoughts, evil imaginings: does this come home to any of us? If so, we belong to the second class Jesus warns.

The Self-deceived

Of the third class were the Pharisees. They are not mentioned in the Old Testament. They emerged during the inter-testamental period at the time of the Maccabean struggle in which they played a heroic and uncompromising role, choosing to die rather than to violate conscience by defending themselves on the Sabbath. The word *Pharisee* means "separated" or "separatist."

The radical English Puritans like the Mayflower Pilgrims were called Separatists. The Pharisee was the Puritan of his day. He was an earnest student of the scriptures, loved to meditate upon them. It was a Pharisee who wrote Psalm 119:

> O, how I love thy law!
> It is my meditation all the day. . . .
> Thy word is a lamp to my feet
> And a light to my path. . . .

The temple, the central shrine at Jerusalem, was the Sadducees' province. The Pharisee devoted himself to the synagogue, the local church. After the destruction of the temple by the Romans in the year 70, the Pharisee preserved Judaism with its lofty monotheism and its high ethical teaching by keeping the synagogues going and establishing new ones throughout the Mediterranean world wherever the Jews scattered.

He was a conscientious tither—a tenth of all that came to him he gave to the Lord. He took seriously the commandment, "Remember the Sabbath day to keep it holy," and drew up an elaborate set of rules to guide him. The world is so full of lax, easy-going folk who have no liking for self-discipline let alone self-denial that I admire those who have standards and try to live up to them even if their standards are not mine. Yet Jesus' most scathing words were spoken to the Pharisee!

The trait commonly associated with him is self-righteousness, self-satisfaction. As long as a man realizes he is not all he ought to be, there is hope for him. When he thinks he is as good as a man needs to be and compares his moral status with others' to their disadvantage, we call him *pharisaical*. So the Pharisee has come into our language.

As Jesus told him, he was self-deceived. He liked to dress in his best clothes and sit in the best seat in the synagogue. When the collection plate was passed, he ostentatiously put in his tithe. He prayed long, repetitious prayers, standing at a main intersection so that men could not fail to see him and be impressed by his piety. He came to think that his prayers and his righteousness were the real thing, that God could not see through them and through him.

He had his perspective wrong, Jesus told him. He tithed mint, dill and other garden herbs, scrupulously putting aside a tenth for the Lord, while he neglected the basic aspects of religion—justice and mercy. He could not distinguish between a mosquito and a camel, straining the mosquito out of his drink while he gulped down the camel.

In the early session minutes of the Old First Church of East Cleveland are records of church discipline. Certain men were suspended from membership and barred from the communion table. They had sold whisky to the Indians. But they were not disciplined for that. They were disciplined because they had sold it on Sunday—they had broken the Sabbath.

Come closer home. Here is a man who prides himself that he neither, smokes nor drinks. But he invests in distillery and cigarette stocks on the theory that since others are addicted to these indulgences he may as well profit by their addiction, especially since he gives a considerable portion of his income to church and charity.

Wrong perspective: that was the trouble with the Pharisee, evicting widows from their houses while sedulously giving his tithe.

He had created a God in his own image whom he naturally expected to fulfill his desires. It was an intellectual sin: the tying in of destiny with self-interest. Instead of praying as Jesus prayed, "Into thy hands I commit my spirit. Not my will but thine be done," he tried to make God a side-partner in promoting his own schemes like a certain John Ward who prayed, "O Lord, have an eye of compassion on the county of Herfordshire for I have a mortgage in that county. Likewise give, I beseech thee, a prosperous voyage to the sloop *Mermaid*, for I have not insured it."

Do you ever pray like that, trying—not so naïvely, of course—to bend God's will to yours, to make him an accomplice in your designs? If so, you belong to the third group which Jesus warns.

Those Who Hear and Talk but Do Not Do

A fourth class whom Jesus excoriates (excoriate is a high-toned word meaning *to strip the hide off*) are those who hear and talk but do not do. Words do not pass into action, knowledge is not sharpened into resolution.

There are two main conceptions of Christianity in the New Testament. They are not in conflict, they are two sides of the same shield. According to Paul, we are saved by grace through faith. That is, we are saved by God's undeserved kindness through acceptance of his offer in Christ, saved not by what we do for God but by what he does for us. This is the doctrine known as justification by faith.

According to the teaching of Jesus as reported in the synoptic gospels, Christianity is a deed. Do you remember how the Sermon on the Mount ends?

> Not everyone who says to me, 'Lord, Lord,' shall enter the kingdom of heaven but he who does the will of my Father who is in heaven.
> Everyone who hears these words of mine and does them will be like a wise man, a sensible man, who built his house upon rock.
> Down came the rain, angrily swirled the flood, fierce blew the wind and beat on that house. But it did not fall. It was built on rock.

Everyone who hears these words and does them not will be like a foolish man who built his house on sand.

Down came the rain, angrily swirled the flood, fierce blew the wind and beat on that house. And it fell. And great was its fall.

We may paraphrase:

Not everyone who hears my ideas [words are symbols of ideas] and admires them, not everyone who hears them and says, "How true," not everyone who hears them and has his feelings moved by them, not everyone who hears them and discusses them, but everyone who hears them and translates them into action—for only as ideas are translated into action are they built into character.

People sometimes say to a preacher, "I enjoyed the sermon," or "Thank you for the sermon," a polite and gracious thing to say. Once in a blue moon someone hears a sermon and acts on it. In a Lenten noonday service I preached on the text, "Let all bitterness, wrath, anger, malice be put away from you and be kind to one another, forgiving one another as God in Christ forgave you" (Ephesians 4:31-32). The sermon was just an excuse to keep repeating the text. Next day a note was left at the hotel: "There was a member of my family from whom I had been estranged. When I heard what you said I knew I had to go to him and get it straightened out. It wasn't easy, but I did it. I thought you might like to know." You can't imagine what a queer feeling it gives a preacher when someone takes him seriously!

Once a sentimental woman said to Jesus, "Blessed is the womb that bore you and the breasts you sucked." Jesus answered, "Blessed rather are those who hear the word of God and keep it." In his interpretation of the Parable of the Sower, he likens those who hear the word but do not do it to seed sown on rock or among thorns—it comes to nothing, produces no fruit. To the faithful servants in the Parable of the Talents their master says, not "Well said," or "Well thought, good and faithful servant," but "Well done."

The statement is widely made that we are having a religious revival. There is an epidemic of church building. There are the photogenic Billy Graham, the euphoric Dr. Peale, the ingratiating Bishop Sheen, each with his large and attentive audience. The leading article in a recent *Saturday Evening Post* was entitled "Religion on the Campus." Its author, a college chaplain, asserts that the colleges are in the midst of a revival of religious faith, cites the increased enrollment in elective courses in religion, the willingness to engage in religious discussion.

I should say that we are having a revival of religious interest rather than a revival of religious faith. Some months ago *Time* ran a feature article on Cleveland. It noted that Cleveland is full of discussion groups, panel discussions, lectures followed by question periods; declared that if a Clevelander were given his choice between going to heaven or discussing heaven, he'd choose the discussion.

Religious discussion is an innocent pastime. It was a favorite with the Athenians of Paul's day (Acts 17:21). But it is one thing to discuss the nature of God, another to commit your way to him. One thing to argue the pros and cons of Job's question, "If a man die, shall he live again?" Another to live here and now as they must live who believe they are immortal with spirits as lasting as God's own.

I am grateful for the revival of religious interest. It may be the prelude to a revival of religious faith. But they are not the same. One consists of hearing and talking, the other of commitment.

> Grant us the will to fashion as we feel,
> Grant us the strength to labor as we know,
> Grant us the purpose, ribbed and edged
>   with steel,
>   To strike the blow.
>
> Knowledge we ask not—knowledge thou
>   has lent,
> But, Lord, the will—there lies our bitter need.
> Give us to build above the deep intent
>   The deed, the deed.

Well may we make John Drinkwater's prayer our own, for hearing and talking without doing, says Jesus, is not only futile, it is a form of self-deception. We think we have accomplished something when we have not.

Does this find any of us? If so, we belong to the fourth group Jesus warned.

Those Who Cannot Make up Their Minds

The last class—those who cannot make up their minds, come to a decision and follow through—is closely akin to the fourth one. James Harvey Robinson in *The Mind in the Making* lists four types of mental activity in ascending order: reverie or day dreaming, casual decisions (which tie shall I wear? what shall I have for lunch?), rationalizing (giving ourselves reasons for doing what we want to do or have already done) and making up our minds.

Jesus put a high value on the ability to make a decision. "No one who puts his hand to the plow and looks back is fit for the kingdom of God." The Greek word *euthetos,* which the versions translate "fit," means literally "ready for use," "easy to place." The indecisive, vacillating, irresolute man is not easy to place in the kingdom of God. What place can there be in a kingdom won on a cross for a man who cannot decide whether to plow or not to plow—who, if he decides to plow, cannot be relied on to reach to the end of the furrow? who starts to build a tower without first counting the cost and making sure he has the resources to complete it, and so has to abandon the project before it is done? Literally, Jesus has no use for such a man. Like the man who kept his talent but did not use it, he is not bad, he is just no good.

Did you ever notice how many of Jesus' parables turn on energy, resolution, decision? The widow who, having lost one of the slowly accumulated hoard of coins she needs to pay her taxes or buy something for her children, says, "I am going to find that coin if I have to turn the house upside down and inside out"; the shepherd who, finding that one of his sheep is missing, goes out into the hills and into the night saying, "I am going to search for that sheep until I find it"; the servants who take the talents entrusted to them and put them to use;

the bridesmaids who think ahead and bring an extra supply of oil in case of emergency; the widow who will have justice if she has to wear the judge down in order to get it; the man who, having found buried treasure, never rests till he has sold all he has and bought the field in which it lay; the man at midnight who keeps pounding at his neighbor's door till he gets the bread he needs to set before his belated guest; the man who is ready to cut off the hand or pluck out the eye that causes him to sin: these are the men and women Jesus admires.

He deplores slackness—the man who promises to work and does not keep his promise, the man who receives a new idea with enthusiasm but whose mind has not depth enough for it to take root and grow, the man who builds on sand. There they were in the days of Noah, he says, eating, drinking, marrying, dreaming, till the floods came and destroyed them.

Does he not put his finger on our trouble—the fickle, wavering weakness of indecision? We have a divided loyalty, can not make up our minds whether to serve God or mammon— we try to serve both despite Jesus' assurance that it can not be done.

Like the rich young ruler, we are attracted to Jesus. But when we are asked to give up something for him, we want time to consider. And often, as with that well-heeled young man, it is our worldly goods that come between us and him. Jesus regarded possessions as a means to an end, not an end in themselves. He disliked and distrusted luxury which distracts the mind, enervates the will and needlessly complicates life.

Samuel Johnson thought that the sensuous delights and rich luxuries of this world are what make death terrible. At least they make life futile and unfit us for the kingdom of God. In a competitive, prestige society, we live like decadent Roman emperors. Our cars are so long we have difficulty parking them, so low we can't sit up straight in them—we slump and get curvature of the spine.

It is possible to be worldly without being gross. When Paul writes sadly of one of his helpers, "Demos forsook me, having loved this present world," he does not mean that Demos had fallen into carnal sin. Paul meant only that when it came to a showdown Demos preferred the tangible prizes, the solid satisfactions of this world. So he missed his chance to have a part in the greatest redemptive movement in history and his life flickered out in disloyalty.

Is not this our danger still? Make these lines of the hymn your daily prayer:

> O Jesus, I have promised to serve thee to the end.
> O give me grace to follow, my master and my friend.

For the irresolute folk, the inconstant, indecisive folk are a fifth class whom Jesus warns.

L'envoi

This has been a serious and none too cheerful theme. But I have reached a point where I no longer play around the fringes. I have no premonitions. But I know what Richard Baxter meant when he said, "I preach as who should never preach again, I preach as dying man to dying men." If you forget everything else in this chapter, this is what I ask you to re-member: he who warns us of the dangers of living came to show us the way out and the way through. He came, he said, to seek and to save. In the nativity story according to Mat-thew, the angel said to Joseph, "You shall call his name Jesus, for he will save his people from their sins." The most un-qualified promise is found in the best known verse of all: "For God so loved the world that he gave his only Son, that who-ever believes in him should not perish but have eternal life. For God did not send his Son into the world to condemn the world but that the world through him might be saved."

> He did not come to judge the world,
> He did not come to blame;
> He did not only come to seek—
>   It was to save he came.
> And when we call him Saviour
> We call him by his name.

The Perpetual Miracle

Sursum Corda

O Thou who hast drawn back the curtain of the night
    to unveil the color and brightness of the morn,
    who hast called us up from the weakness and uncon-
        sciousness of sleep to the light and joy of another day,
    who with each new day dost renew the opportunity
        to live, to learn, to love, to serve,
    let the hush of thy presence fall upon us,
    lift up our hearts as we lift them up to thee.

Loose us from the worries and distractions that harass us,
    the dull and sullen moods that depress us,
    the trivial and earth-bound thoughts that come
        between us and thee.

Let some sure word from thee get through to us who
        need thee,
    lead us step by step into the deep places of the Spirit
        where Christ may speak to us of thee,
    and all that is within us will bless thy holy name. Amen.

THE PERPETUAL MIRACLE
A Study of Matthew 16:13-25

JESUS' CONVERSATION with his disciples at Caesarea Philippi marks the turning point in his career. It occurred near the end of his life, shortly before he set out on his last journey to Jerusalem. His star, which had reached its zenith during his Galilean ministry, had begun to set. The people who had flocked to him in the belief that he would overthrow the Roman power and restore national independence had deserted him when it became evident that he did not intend to lead an insurrection against Rome. His popularity had waned. His enemies were closing in. He had aroused the powerful opposition of the synagogue party, the Pharisees, and the equally formidable opposition of the temple party, the Sadduces. Herod Antipas, whose guilty conscience made him fear that Jesus was John the Baptist come back to life, was trying to catch and kill him.

Unable to continue his work in Galilee, he retreated northward to a secluded region where he could give himself to prayer, summoning all his resources and resolution to meet the dread ordeal which lay before him, and to training his disciples. No longer speaking to throngs, he concentrated on the twelve men on whom he relied to carry on when he was gone. They had known him as a good comrade, magnetic teacher, popular hero. Now he was a fugitive, discredited by the leaders of the nation, rejected by the people. They had seen him unspoiled by success. Now they saw him undaunted by failure.

The conversation at Caesarea Philippi was the culmination of a period of intensive training. The crisis in Galilee had brought out aspects of his character and his interpretation of his mission which the disciples did not fully understand. Note that Jesus, like all first-rate teachers, was a skilled questioner, asking questions which would draw them out and lead up to what he wanted them to know. It was he who introduced the subject which led up to Peter's confession by asking, "Who do men say that I am?" He asked it not from morbid self-consciousness such as vain men feel about others' opinion of them. He asked it to elicit an expression of their faith in him because he was about to speak to them of something which would try their faith—his sufferings which they must share.

They answered, "Men are not agreed. Some say John the Baptist, some Elijah, some Jeremiah or another of the prophets." Knowing the veneration in which the prophets were held, one would suppose this estimate would satisfy anyone. It did not satisfy Jesus. He may have been gratified by it but he did not accept it. The meek and lowly Nazarene, even then despised and rejected by men, was not content to be classed with even the greatest of the prophets. Peering earnestly into their faces, he asked, "Who do you say that I am?"

Peter gave the answer his faith and love impelled, "You are the Christ, the son of the living God."

Jesus never spoke with stronger emotion than in his response to Peter's words. We can see how deeply they moved him, how grateful he was for them: "Blessed are you, Simon: for flesh and blood have not revealed this to you but my Father in heaven." In other words, no one taught you this, you didn't get it from books or men or by the unaided effort of your own mind; it was given to you by God.

Did Jesus Intend to Found a Church?

The meaning of Jesus' next words has been in dispute from that day to this: "You are Peter, and on this rock I will build my church and the gates of hell [thus the King James Version; the Revised Standard Version reads, 'the powers of death'] shall not prevail against it."

By the time Matthew was written, about 85, *ecclesia*** (which the English versions translate "church") had long been the title of the Christian society. We find it often in the Acts, the letters of Paul and the Revelation. It occurs also in Hebrews, James, I Peter and III John. Only twice is Jesus reported to have used it, both times in Matthew unsupported by the other gospels—and "special Matthew," that is, material unique to Matthew, is regarded as the least reliable of

* Whence our words "ecclesiastic," "ecclesiastical." It means literally "those called," an assembly duly convened. It was the word the Greeks used of the town meetings of their city states. When Jerome (ca. 380) translated the Greek New Testament into Latin, he rendered *ecclesia* by the Latin word *congregatio,* "congregation."

the four sources underlying the synoptic gospels.* In the other instance (Matthew 18:17, which deals with a matter of church discipline) it obviously reflects a later situation, the situation at the time Matthew was written, fifty years after Jesus' death. Hence questions have arisen: Did Jesus use the word "church"? Did he intend to found a church? I have no difficulty in supposing that he used an Aramaic word signifying a religious community—the church idea goes back as far as Isaiah—which the evangelist translated by the Greek word *ecclesia*.

The question, Did Jesus intend to found a church? is academic. Whether or not he founded it in a formal sense, the church began when in Mark's simple words "he called to him those whom he desired and they came; and he appointed twelve to be with him and to be sent out to preach."

These twelve he welded into a compact group, gave them his ruling ideas in a form they could memorize and teach to others, and encouraged and trained them to enlarge their group by winning others to it. By the Day of Pentecost, often called the birthday of the church, fifty days after the resurrection, the twelve had grown to one hundred twenty. On that day as a result of Peter's bold and persuasive preaching three thousand were won. "And the Lord added to them day by day those who were being saved."

But the church's most rapid growth came in the last century. Professor Kenneth S. Latourette of Yale in his seven-volume *A History of the Expansion of Christianity* devotes

---

* The other three are Mark, the "sayings source" used by both Mark and Luke, and "special Luke."

the same space—three volumes—to the single century 1815-1914 (from the Congress of Vienna which followed the Napoleonic Wars to the outbreak of World War I) that he gives to the eighteen centuries preceding. In the nineteenth century the modern missionary movement was born. As a result Christianity has become in the truest sense a world religion, more widespread geographically than it or any other religion has ever been.

For centuries Christians prayed for church unity, echoing our Lord's prayer "that they may all be one." Now through the World Council they are trying to realize their prayer. The Christian church is the one unbreakable world organism which overpasses national boundaries and has survived two world wars. When our soldiers and sailors landed on lonely, isolated islands, in tropic jungles, in frozen arctic wastes, they found the church at work there. On the last night of Jesus' life he gathered the Twelve for a farewell meal. All that we see of the church in the world today has come out of this little company, gathered about a table in an upstairs room, hearing their leader say, "This is my body. This is my blood. This do in remembrance of me."

What Did Jesus Mean by "This Rock"?

"You are Peter and on this rock I will build my church." The second controversial word in the sentence is "rock." Who or what did Jesus mean by "this rock"? Did he mean Peter? This is the official answer of the Roman Church which therefore bases the church historically on Peter, exalts him above

the other apostles, names the largest cathedral in Christendom
for him and claims him as the first pope, the first head of the
visible church, asserting that the man who lives in the Vatican
today is his lineal successor, the vicar of Christ to whom are
given the keys of heaven and the authority to bind and loose.

An attempt has been made from the Protestant side to
counter this dogma by pointing out that while Peter's name
(*Petros*) is masculine, the usual Greek word for rock (*petra*)
is feminine. This might have weight if Jesus were speaking in
Greek, but there is every reason to think that he was speaking in his own tongue, for throughout the passage the Aramaic
shows through the Greek. "Bar-Jona"—*bar* is the Aramaic
word for son. "Flesh and blood," "my Father who is in
heaven," "the gates of hell*," "the keys of the kingdom of
heaven": these are all Aramaic or Hebraic idioms. In Aramaic
there is no distinction of gender. The word Jesus used was
Cephas, the Aramaic word for rock. It was Peter's nickname,
given him by Jesus (Mark 3:16, "Simon whom he surnamed
Peter"). This Protestant argument is weak.

Yet even Catholics are not agreed that the rock is Peter.
The Catholic scholar Launoy reckons that seventeen of the
Church Fathers regard Peter as the rock; sixteen (including
St. Augustine) think Jesus is the rock; eight believe that Jesus
meant all the apostles and that therefore the church is built
on them all**; forty-four—a majority—believe that the rock
is Peter's confession. With this last interpretation I agree.

---

* That is, *Sheol*, the abode of the dead, which the Hebrews conceived as a
subterranean region enveloped in thick darkness.

** Perhaps influenced by Revelation 21:14.

I do not think Jesus meant that the rock was Peter. Surely he did not mean to confer on Peter any such primacy as the Roman Church has accorded him. His position while he lived was far from that of pope. After Jesus' death his brother James superseded Peter as head of the primitive church. In the church council described in Acts 15 where an important issue was decided—that gentiles need not be circumcised (that is, become Jews) in order to become Christians—James presided. Peter played an influential but subordinate role. In Acts 11 Peter is sharply if unfairly criticized for baptizing a Roman officer named Cornelius and obliged to defend himself before the church. In II Corinthians 11:5 Paul claims for himself an authority equal to Peter's, though he had never seen Jesus in the flesh. In Galatians 2:11 he tells how he once withstood Peter and rebuked him to his face. Nor did Peter claim pre-eminence for himself. In the first letter which bears his name he refers to himself as "a fellow elder"—one of the brethren.*

This is not to belittle Peter. His real primacy is based on his character, courage and ability. Until the church was well under way it was he who led the advance at every step. He led the Twelve in recognizing Jesus as Messiah. He rallied them after the resurrection. He guided the church in its first

* Most scholars regard I Peter as pseudonymous. However, it may well have been written by Silvanus (I Pet. 5:12. Silvanus was probably Silas, Paul's companion on his missionary journeys) who, regarding himself as Peter's spokesman, felt justified in ascribing it to him. He may have written it while Peter was alive and under his supervision, though in its present form it is probably later. The "fiery ordeal" it speaks of (I Pet. 4:12) may be the Neronic persecution of 64 or the Domitian persecution of 95.

decision when Matthias was chosen to replace Judas. He gave the church a voice on the Day of Pentecost. He braced and rallied his fellow Christians in time of persecution. He shepherded the outlying churches of Palestine. Later he went to Antioch, the second great Christian center (Jerusalem being the first), where the Greek mission began. Finally he reached Rome, the imperial city. There, according to an early and strong tradition, both he and Paul lost their lives in the Neronic persecution. His denial of Jesus is a black mark on his record but, had he not risked his life to keep contact with Jesus after his arrest, he would not have been recognized and challenged. It is no accident that his name comes first in every list of the Twelve in the New Testament (Mark 3:16; Matthew 10:2; Luke 6:14; Acts 1:13). It is no wonder that when Paul three years after his conversion went to Jerusalem, he went to visit Peter (Galatians 1:18). With his keen eyes he saw in Peter the man who could tell him the facts about Jesus he needed to know.

It was a daring venture of faith and love for a Jew with his ingrained monotheism to express for the first time the conviction that Jesus was in a unique sense the Son of God. In Jesus' grateful response Peter had his reward. Maybe it was to Peter's character that Jesus referred as though to say, "It is on character like yours, faulty to be sure but with something granitic about it, it is on loyalty like yours I will build my church." But I do not think Jesus meant that the rock was Peter.

Nor do I think Jesus referred to himself as the rock on which his church was to be built, though we so speak of him. True, we sing of him as "the great rock foundation whereon our feet were set by sovereign grace," remembering Paul's assertion that "other foundation can no one lay than that which is laid, which is Jesus Christ." True, he applied to himself in another connection (the Parable of the Vineyard) these words from Psalm 118: "The stone which the builders rejected is become the head of the corner." But I do not think Jesus here spoke of himself.

No, I believe he referred to Peter's confession. A living man professing a living faith in Jesus as the Christ, the son of the living God: this is the rock on which the church is built. One of the most influential thinkers of our time, Paul Tillich, says that Christianity was born not with the birth of Jesus but at the moment when Peter was impelled to say of him, "You are the Christ."*

It is impossible to say what this meant to Peter** but to us it means at least two things. First, the conviction that in Jesus

* *Systematic Theology,* vol. 2, Existence and the Christ, page 97.

** The Greek word *Christ* can be translated into the Hebrew word *Messiah,* which means "the anointed one." The reasons which led Peter to identify Jesus with the Messiah are not easy to give, for Jesus does not fit any picture of the Messiah to be found in Jewish prophecy or apocalypse. He does fit the picture of the Suffering Servant in Isaiah 53, a passage which profoundly influenced his own conception of his mission, but scholars do not regard Isaiah 53 as Messianic. It was probably under the spell of Jesus' moral majesty and the conviction that his and the other disciples' relation to God was bound up with their relation to Jesus that Peter seized the highest term he could think of and applied it to him. Jesus at once pledged the disciples to silence: they were to keep the Messianic secret. Thomas De Quincey thinks that what Judas betrayed to the authorities was not *where* Jesus was (which they could easily have found out for themselves) but *who* he was—the Messiah.

How and when Jesus himself came to the realization that he was the Messiah we do not know. The most baffling of all problems concerning Jesus is his own self-consciousness. When and how did he become aware of his unique relation to God? Was it borne in upon him gradually, or did it come in a sudden flash of insight, perhaps at his baptism?

we have not only a comrade, teacher and friend but also a saviour—one who gives us both an adequate ideal and the power to work toward it. Second, the conviction that God is like his anointed one on earth. This is an even more daring venture of faith: to project into the infinite and eternal the character of Jesus; to believe that the mind and heart of a universe which often seems uncaring, sometimes sinister and cruel, are like the mind and heart of Jesus; to believe that the God who created and controls the universe is the eternal cross-bearer—the God whose heart beats in sympathy with ours, who loves us through all our sins and will love us out of them if we will let him, of whose love Calvary is the measure and the sign. Can you believe that Jesus perfectly discloses the character of God? This is what it means to profess that he is the Christ.

The Supreme Miracle

When this conviction comes to a man it is a miracle—meaning by miracle not something that involves a breach with natural law but something that transcends natural law. I count it the supreme miracle of the New Testament. Greater than the feeding of the multitude, or the raising of Jairus' daughter, or the healing of the man born blind, is this miracle wrought at Caesarea Philippi when Peter cried, "You are the Christ, the Son of the living God."

Unless this miracle is continually reproduced the church will fail. As long as men, seeing Jesus, are impelled to cry, "You are the Christ, the Son of the living God," the church will endure and against it the gates of hell will not prevail. The purpose of the church is to create the atmosphere in which this miracle may be wrought. The church is more than a humanitarian society or a fraternal order or an ethical cult; it is the community of those who believe that Jesus is the Christ, the Son of the living God and who bear witness to their faith before the world.

How do we get this conviction? Flesh and blood will not reveal it to us any more than to Peter. We cannot prove it. It is one of the unproved truths by which men live. We cannot reach it by study or discussion or repeating the creeds. It finds expression in the creeds. But it will never take possession of us until it comes to us as it came to Peter as a flash of light from heaven.

Yet I would not have you think that there is anything magical about it or that it comes by chance or is reserved to some spiritual aristocracy and denied to the rest. It is a miracle which will be wrought in anyone who fulfills the conditions. You do what he asks you to do—learn of him, follow him, work, serve, pray with him. Someday the conviction will be born in you that this Jesus with whom you have worked and prayed is all in all.

The church is founded upon this miracle and exists to foster the atmosphere of faith and love in which it may recur. It is not necessary that you experience it before you come into the church or have a right to call yourself a Christian. A Christian is a disciple, a follower, one who keeps on trying to follow Jesus. But you never enter into the fullness of the Christian life till you come to your Caesarea Philippi when your heart cries, "This Jesus is the Christ, the anointed one of God, to me."

One Saturday evening many years ago I was putting the finishing touches on an Easter sermon. It was on a text from the Revelation, "I am the first and the last and the living one; I died and am alive forevermore." I had used a historical illustration: how, when the storm clouds were gathering about him, Luther traced in the dust on a table top the word *vivit*, kept repeating softly to himself *vivit*—"he lives." I had used a biblical illustration: how Jesus eight days after his resurrection had come to his disciples, gathered again in the upstairs room; how he had given skeptical Thomas convincing proof of his reality; how the miracle was wrought in Thomas so that he cried, "My lord and my God!"

As I read over the sermon it came to me as though for the first time that *Jesus is alive*. I had always believed that in theory; I had never doubted his ability to transcend death. But I had thought of him vaguely as living with God and continuing here as an influence, an example. I had never seen the bearing of his being alive on me. Then it came to me like a flash that he can be to me all that he was to Peter, James and John; can do for me all he did for them, enable me to do the hard things I have to do, keep me from doing the things that would spoil my life; that he is not only the saviour of the world, he is my saviour. Our Episcopal brethren believe in the real presence of Christ in the sacrament. I believe in the real presence of Christ all the time, that (as Whittier sings) "warm, sweet, tender, even yet a present help is he; and faith has still its Olivet and love its Galilee." So that I don't have to die to win. I've won already. I don't have to die to be with him. I'm with him now.

The Arch Heresy

This would be a good place to stop. We are on the summit, anything more must be a descent. But Jesus did not stop with his moving response to Peter's confession. He went on to speak for the first time of his cross, linked his Christhood with his death as though to say, "This is the kind of Messiah I am. This is how I must save the world." "Then said Jesus to his disciples, 'If any man will come after me, let him deny himself and take up his cross and follow me.'"

This is how we confirm our faith and bear witness to it before the world: by becoming fellow cross-bearers with him. This is the proof of our belief in him, not our willingness to repeat the Nicene formula about him—"Very God of very God, begotten not made; of one substance with the Father"— but our willingness to take up our cross daily and follow him. Easy to say it. Would that we had strength to live it! Merely to say it is to humble us and make us cry out to him to give us strength to be true to our conviction about him.

For this is the arch heresy: to believe in Jesus and disbelieve in his method of saving the world; to be convinced that he is the Christ and unwilling to pay the price of that conviction; to call him lord and still, despite all that has happened, put our trust in the things in which the world puts its trust—gold, steel, atomic-driven submarines, intercontinental missiles, power politics, "massive retaliation"—as though they will save the world. This is the heresy of our time, and we are all guilty of it.

Peter fell into the same pit. He made his great confession, received Jesus' glowing praise, then expected an easy time. "God forbid, Lord! This shall never happen to you," he said when Jesus began to speak of his cross. Praise turned to stern rebuke as Jesus answered, "Get behind me! You are a hindrance to me, for you are not on the side of God but of men." How often must he say that to us who confess that he is the Christ, the saviour of the world, but shrink from following through on that conviction, from applying his teaching not only to ourselves but to the troubled areas where men's wills and passions clash.

Three points then in this scene we have been studying, the turning point in Jesus' ministry: first, the revelation; second, the confession; third, the consecration, the cost.

O God, may the miracle be wrought in us so that we too are impelled to cry, "My Saviour, my Lord!"—then accept the consequence, share in his saviourhood, and take up our own crosses.

Only so will his grace abide with us always. Amen.

What Jesus Says About Man

His Hand to Guide

Help us to prove worthy of our Lord's confidence in us, never to disappoint his high hopes for us or rest content in any lower thought of ourselves.

With his strong hand to guide us, his bracing words to encourage us, may we climb the heights to which he points us till we too attain mature manhood, to the measure of the stature of the fullness of Christ.

Of whom else can we ask so much, especially when we ask it in his name? Amen.

WHAT JESUS SAYS ABOUT MAN

THE FOURTH GOSPEL says of Jesus that "he needed no one to bear witness of man, for he knew what was in man"; or as Moffatt translates, "He required no evidence from anyone about human nature; well did he know what was in human nature."

Time has justified this claim. None of us fully understands Jesus, but as we turn the pages of the gospels we find ourselves in the presence of one who understands us, one "to whom all hearts are open, all desires known, and from whom no secrets are hid."

He knew the seamy side of human nature, its depths as well as its heights. When President Roosevelt returned from the Teheran Conference, he was asked his impression of Marshall Stalin. "He is the same kind of man I am: a realist," he said. Whether President Roosevelt was realistic in his negotiations with Stalin is in retrospect open to question. But the word fits Jesus. What is a realist? The opposite of a romanticist or a sentimentalist; one who looks facts in the face, not through rose-colored glasses and not through saffron-colored glasses either.

What is Jesus' verdict on man? Let me remind you of five statements he makes. I shall not quote him verbatim but shall give the clear sense of his words.

The Deepest Thing in Man Is His Likeness to God

Jesus does not blink facts. He does not say that human nature is altogether beautiful, that everybody wants to be good, is trying to be good, would be good if he had the chance. This is what he says: "From within, out of man's heart, come evil thoughts, fornication, theft, murder, adultery, coveting, wickedness, deceit, licentiousness, slander, pride, foolishness." All this brood of devils comes out of the heart. He also said of a man out of whom such devils had come that when he came to himself he said, "I will arise and go to my father." He had played the fool, but when his manhood reasserted itself he said, "I am going back where I belong." The deepest thing in him was his kinship with his father.

Near the end of his life, knowing men would nail him to a cross, Jesus said, "I, if I be lifted up, will draw all men to me." When they see the lengths to which my love will go, they will respond. Human nature is so constituted they can't help it.

We can see that man is often stupid and selfish, sometimes brutal and cruel, "a cross between the jackal and the jackass" as Mr. Mencken said. Anyone can see that. It has always been easy to be cynical about man for he has always given ample scope for cynicism. Jesus knew what was in man. He says that the deepest thing is divine.

A Man Can Change

Some dispute this: "You can't make a silk purse out of a sow's ear." Many of our leading novelists and playwrights are pessimistic about human nature. Their characters are not victors but victims, not so much acting as acted upon, creatures of circumstance, victims of fate, incapable of choice, incapable of change. This is not the traditional American attitude which, as it finds expression in Jefferson, Franklin, Emerson, Whitman and William James, is that man can not only reshape his world, he can reshape himself in the process.

And it is not the attitude of the New Testament which from first to last assumes that human nature can and must be changed. It was not to a callow youth but to a leading citizen, a man of mature years, that Jesus said, "You must be born anew." Nicodemus is skeptical: "How can a man be born when he is old?" But Jesus insists he can. Paul, writing to the church in Corinth, lists the most depraved and dissolute elements in that notoriously corrupt city—men and women guilty of unspeakable vice. "Some of you used to be like that," he says, "but you were changed." He could never forget how he himself had been faced about, made over again. "Wherefore," he says, "if any man is in Christ he is a new creation."

In our day the New Testament has received strong confirmation at this point from the savants. Professor E. L.

Thorndike on the basis of exhaustive tests in the field of adult education refutes the old adage, "You can't teach an old dog new tricks," asserting we can go on learning new tricks as long as we live. A psychiatrist of high standing wrote an article entitled "Why People Change" for *Harper's*. Reading it discloses that he is not sure why people change but takes it for granted they do. He cites Paul, St. Augustine, St. Francis of Assisi, and Leo Tolstoi as conspicuous examples.

In a day when the church says little about conversion and regeneration lest it be thought old-fashioned, psychologists such as Overstreet, Adler and Hadfield stress psychological rebirth as the process by which life advances from stage to stage. "This," says Dr. Hadfield, famed neurologist, "is what Nicodemus could not understand. As a man of the world he did not believe one can change human nature, forgetting that human nature does nothing but change." Do you remember what Dr. Dorsey says in *Why We Behave Like Human Beings*? "Man's really distinguishing trait is his capacity for modifiable behavior."

Habits are deep-rooted, but by introducing new and stronger motives they can be changed. In Alcoholics Anonymous are hundreds of walking examples. The thought life, the emotional life, the imagination can be brought under control. Defects of temperament are not to be taken lying down but struggled against with might and main as one would struggle against any other handicap that kept him from fullest power. We can even undertake the re-education of the will with every prospect of success.

What psychology is telling us now the New Testament has been saying all along. If a man is in a rut he need not stay there. If he has a bad disposition he can change it into a good disposition. If he is dissatisfied with his moral status he need not stay as he is.

Man Can Conquer All His Enemies

We hear it said that environment conditions a man's character, leaves its mark upon him, determines his destiny. The influence of environment is strong—which is why we want not only our children but all children to have a fostering environment in their impressible years.

As we grow older we can select from our environment the elements we want to play upon our lives and shut the door on the rest. We can choose most of our associations, the causes to which we give ourselves, the groups to which we belong. With some of us, books—next to our family and friends—are the most influential factor in our environment. We are free to choose what books we read.

If there are untoward factors in our environment from which we cannot escape, we can stand up to them and assert our integrity against them. A man's environment is important. What he does in face of it is more important. He need not supinely acquiesce and conform. A few years ago it was the fashion to say that the object of education was to adjust the individual to his environment. True. But education should also teach the individual to resist his environment when necessary or those elements in it which would drag him down, to "be not conformed to this world."

Others hold that heredity is what loads the dice. Everything depends on your ancestors. "Blood will tell." Of course it will tell—a clean heredity is not to be despised—but it will not tell everything. This fatalistic idea cuts the nerve of effort, weakens the sense of personal accountability. "What's the use? Mendel's Law settled it. Germ plasma is fate. If it isn't in the genes, there's nothing you can do." A man remembers the diseases his forebears died of; worse still, their moral weaknesses. Autosuggestion does the rest. If he sees any symptoms of them cropping out in him he is tempted to say, "I was made that way," and give up the fight.

Suppose Lincoln with his deep vein of melancholy had known as much about genetics as we do. Can you not hear him brooding? "The cards were stacked against me. I was licked before I was born. My father was a lazy ne'er-do-well, my mother a good but commonplace woman. There's no culture, let alone genius, in the family. Not only my heredity but my environment was against me. I grew up in frontier conditions of the crudest sort. No wonder I'm crude myself. If I had background and breeding like Charles Sumner's or Robert E. Lee's, I might amount to something." Fortunately he lived before this modern fatalism prevailed. Despite the unpromising material given him he made of himself quite a man.

Environment and heredity have something to say about a man's destiny. But in addition the man has something to say. He casts the deciding vote. The plain teaching of the New

Testament is that a man can conquer all his enemies. He can defeat them, every one.

Nothing Can Hurt a Man but Himself

Any man can hurt himself but no one else can hurt him. Jesus was not the first to say this. Four hundred years earlier lived Socrates—I suppose we should call him a pagan, yet in some respects his life was like our Lord's. Like Jesus, he went about doing good and teaching good and men killed him for his pains. But he met death unembittered. As he sat in his cell in the Mamertine prison awaiting execution he said to his disciples, "No evil can touch a good man, living or dead. They can beat upon this tenement. Socrates they cannot touch."

Said Jesus to his disciples, "They will scourge you. They will put you in prison. Some of you will lose your lives. But no one can harm you. No one can put limits to the reach and range of your personality. No one can subtract from the fullness of your joy. In your inner life you can live above the battle. You have resources within you that the world cannot touch. Moreover, no dirt thrown on you from outside can defile you. The only dirt that defiles is what comes from within. Nothing can hurt or thwart or degrade a man but himself."

Death Does Not Take from a Man Anything Worth Keeping

This is a logical conclusion from the statements already given.

In the farewell discourse of Socrates as reported by Plato we find long, abstruse arguments for immortality. Jesus never argued for immortality. To him it was a corollary of the fatherhood of God. To the Sadducees, who strongly disbelieved in it, he said, "You are quite wrong. God is not God of the dead but of the living, for all live to him." There is more consolation in those simple, forthright words than in all the classic arguments for immortality. They have behind them the weight of his character and the seal of his own triumph over death.

As to the manner of his resurrection there is room for difference of opinion. There were no witnesses. It had already occurred when the women reached Joseph of Arimathea's garden. Was it physical, as the gospels lead us to think with their emphasis on the empty tomb? Or spiritual, as Paul implies in I Corinthians 15? Paul's testimony is earlier. Mark, our earliest gospel, was written about the year 70. Paul wrote I Corinthians not later than 55. He does not mention the empty tomb but lists six occasions when the risen Christ appeared to his followers, the last being when he appeared to Paul himself.

However we explain it, the resurrection will remain a mystery until we know more about the nature of the unseen world and how one who has entered it can make contact with us who are still here. Did Jesus appear to his disciples' eyes or to their faith? In either case he made them sure he was alive, sure his life was so bound in with theirs that because he lived they would live—and live with him.

On this conviction the church was built. The statement

has been made that the church and the New Testament created belief in the resurrection. Any competent historian will
tell you that the exact opposite is true: belief in the resurrection created the church and the New Testament. Without
that belief they would not have been.

Phillips Brooks said he had two main reasons for believing
in God. First, the universe is intelligible with that belief, unintelligible without it. Second, Jesus believed in God, and he
thought Jesus knew. Are not these our two best reasons for
believing in immortality? The long process of evolution, the
growing pains, the withheld completions of this life, make
sense if this life flows out into another; do not make sense if
death is the end. Jesus believed in it and we have reason to
think he knew, he who lived so close to God that those who
knew him best could hardly tell where he left off and God
began. "God is not God of the dead but of the living, for all
live to him." He does not make us to throw us away like
rubbish. Whom he loves, he loves forevermore.

Death is an incident in the process of unfolding life. Death
is a shadow that falls athwart the current of a flowing stream.
Death is the opening of a door that gives access to a life of
larger scope and rapture and permanence than this earth can
afford. Death divests us of extraneous things. We have to
leave them behind. But the things worth keeping—the good
we have done, the character we have won, the love we have
received and given—these we carry with us to the world to
which we go.

"So we do not lose heart. Though our outer nature is wast-
ing away, our inner nature is renewed every day . . . because

we look not to the things that are seen but to the things that are unseen; for the things that are seen are transient, but the things that are unseen are eternal.

"When the perishable puts on the imperishable and the mortal puts on immortality, then shall come to pass the saying that is written, 'Death is swallowed up in victory'. . . . Therefore, my beloved brethren, be steadfast, immovable, always abounding in the work of the Lord, knowing that your labor is not in vain."

What Jesus Says About God

Not Two but One

Infinite and eternal Spirit to whom our spirits are akin,
    on whom at every moment we depend;
    who art not far from any one of us
    for in thee we live and move and have our being
    whenever our lives reach up to their highest and best;
    who has set eternity in our hearts
    that short of thee we can ne'er be satisfied;
    who dost beset us behind and before,
    yet dost wait for our invitation,
    never forcing an entrance to our souls:
Help us to see that the life of man and the life of God
    are not two but one;
    that a man never comes to himself
    until he comes to thee.
"Thou madest us for thyself, O God,
    and our hearts are restless
    until they rest in thee." Amen.

WHAT JESUS SAYS ABOUT GOD

"WILL YOU PLEASE tell me in a few simple words that I can pass on to my boys," asked a high school teacher of his minister, "who, what and where is God?"

Once a man told me the story of his spiritual pilgrimage. He had been brought up in church and had attended more or less until middle life. Then, as a result of a nervous affliction, he had turned to a healing cult, becoming an ardent devotee. In the church, he said, he had never been given an idea of God he could grasp. This cult has given him a conception of God that is definite and clear. Maybe too definite and clear. As someone has said, "God never sat for his photograph."

Yet there may be ground for this man's complaint that the church gives its people inadequate instruction about God. It may be that this is why the thought of the church is impoverished, its power of feeling sluggish and thin, why many good Christian people have vague, childish, even pagan ideas of God.

But only God is permanently interesting. Short of him our minds cannot stop. Beyond him they cannot go. There comes a time, said Eugene O'Neill, when we must make friends with God or we shall have no friend at all, not even ourselves. It is a word to ponder as we grow older and one by one our friends precede us, leaving the world a lonely place. When the lights grow dim and we enter the valley of the shadow, if we know "a friend that sticketh closer than a brother," we shall not walk alone. "We and God were made for one another," said William James, "and in opening ourselves to his influence our highest destiny is fulfilled."

"Tell me in simple words who, what and where is God." In our still moments when deep calls to deep this is what we want to know: what is the nature of the Being from whom we come, to whom we return, on whom at every moment we depend?

Various Ideas of God

If each gave his own answer, we should find how many and diverse are our thoughts of God. As the word *home* calls up a different image to every mind, so with the word God.

What do you think of when you hear it? a venerable figure with a flowing white beard sitting up among the clouds, as Zeus dwelt on Mt. Olympus? or a force like electricity, energizing all things, coursing through all things? or a synonym for life, life that shows itself in the beauty of a tree or in growing crops on a farm or in men and women who are born, reproduce their kind and die?

Or do you think of God as does a distinguished professor, as a personification of our loyalties, like Alma Mater or Uncle Sam? or with another philosopher as the principle of concretion—the principle by which the universe is held together? or with a widely read psychologist as a projection of the father image?

Or with Matthew Arnold as "a power not ourselves that makes for righteousness"? or with Wordsworth as "a presence that disturbs me with the joy of elevated thoughts . . . whose dwelling is the light of setting suns"? or with Santayana as "the soul's invincible surmise"? or with Herbert Carruth as a process, like the process of emergent evolution?

> A fire mist and a planet,
> A crystal and a cell,
> A jelly fish and a saurian,
> And caves where the cave men dwell;
> Then a sense of law and beauty
> And a face turned from the clod—
> Some call it Evolution
> And others call it God.

Or do you think of God as a person who thinks and plans and loves, who shares his life with you and wants you to share your life with him?

Bible Ideas of God

It is not surprising that we have varying ideas of God for there are different ideas in the Bible. In the New Testament we are given the highest idea of God anywhere to be found. But this is the end of a long journey, the most thrilling journey ever made by the mind of man. If you want to follow its successive stages, you will find them charted in Harry Emerson Fosdick's *A Guide to Understanding the Bible*. It is not an easy book. It is a study book. You won't get much out of it by skimming it from the depths of an easy chair. It is the kind of book you have to read sitting in a straight chair at a desk with pencil in hand. But it is not beyond the reach of any intelligent person.

In it Dr. Fosdick shows how the Hebrews found their way from a local, tribal god to the sovereign creator of the universe; from a vengeful god, pleased when prisoners taken in battle were sacrificed to him, as when Samuel "hewed Agag (the Amalakite king) in pieces before the Lord," to a god of compassion—"in all their afflictions he was afflicted"; from a mountain god of war and storm to a universal spirit, everywhere available, the one God of all mankind. So this uniquely gifted people prepared the way for the God of the New Testament whom Paul describes as "the God and Father of our Lord Jesus Christ," of whom he declares, "It is the God who said, 'Let light shine out of darkness'"—you recognize the quotation as from the first page of Genesis—"It is the same God who at creation said, 'Let light shine out of darkness,' who has shone in our hearts to give the light of the knowledge of his glory in the face of Christ."

Paul makes a good point there. In a course which I once taught, the students were required to read Fosdick's *Guide*, then take a test on it. Sometimes they made such statements as this: "When the Hebrews settled in Palestine, Yahweh (the Hebrews' name for their god) became agricultural, blended with the Canannitish baals. Later he became god of the sky, his territory was extended. With Elijah he became a god of social justice. In the New Testament God became Christlike."

They knew what they meant. They meant that in the people's thought Yahweh had become an agricultural deity, and so on. But I reminded them—and at the same time myself—that so far as we know God is what he has always been, has always been what he is. A New Testament writer calls him, "the Father of lights with whom is no variation." Another insists that though we often act out of character, fall below our best, God's character is consistent: "Even if our faith fails he remains true, for he cannot be false to himself."

H. G. Wells and other amateur theologians have proposed a changing God to match a changing universe, an evolving God to correspond with an evolving universe. But this raises more questions than it answers. No, it is man's idea of God that has changed as more light has come to him. God never was a tribal god, a vengeful god, a warrior god, backing one tribe against another. He has always been a Christlike God, the Father of mankind, the high and holy one who inhabits eternity and whose name is holy but who finds his chosen dwelling in the humble, contrite heart.

What Jesus Says About God

Whatever God is, what he means to you will depend on your thought of him, your attitude toward him. The end and aim of every high form of religion is, be like God, reproduce in yourself the divine motives, the divine character. It makes a difference what kind of God we try to be like. Not all ideas of him are equally good, worthy, true. We need a norm, a standard, like the yardstick in the Bureau of Standards in Washington by which all other yardsticks are tested.

In the best-known, best-loved chapter of the New Testament, the fourteenth chapter of John, we are told that on the last night of Jesus' life Philip said to him, "Lord, tell us what God is like. Show us the Father and we shall be satisfied." Jesus answered, "He who has seen me has seen the Father." The same qualities they see in him—his love for them, his desire to help them, his willingness to suffer for them—are what God is eternally.

But in the same chapter Jesus goes on to say, "The Father is greater than I." This thought must be put with the other to complete it. God is like Jesus but greater. All of God that can be disclosed in human life is disclosed in Jesus. But Jesus does not exhaust the meaning of God.

Someone has likened the relation between God and Jesus to that between the ocean and the bay. The ocean and the bay flow into one another. You cannot draw a sharp line and say, "Here the ocean ends and the bay begins." The water of the ocean is like the water of the bay. If you take a specimen of each and submit it to analysis, you will find that their properties are identical.

But you cannot form a complete idea of the ocean by looking out across the bay. There are depths and vastnesses in the ocean that you never know until you have crossed it and been on it in a storm. And you never know the bay until you have seen the ocean pouring in until high water mark is reached and all the estuaries and inlets are full and the bay contains as much of the ocean as can possibly get into it. Jesus contains as much of God as can get into a human life. There are depths and vastnesses in God which Jesus leaves unplumbed. But here is the point: just as there is nothing in the water of the ocean unlike the water of the bay, there is nothing in God which is not congruous with Jesus.

So we turn to Jesus with Philip's request, "Tell us what God is like." We think if anyone can tell us it is he. Here are four statements he made about God. I shall not argue them nor advance them tentatively as theories. This is what the supreme spiritual genius of mankind says is true about God.

God Is Spirit

"God is a spirit." So the older versions translate. But the Greek language has no indefinite article and the new version is correct, "God is spirit." He is here and he is everywhere. Don't try to localize him as the early Hebrews did Yahweh on Mt. Sinai or the Greeks did Zeus on Mt. Olympus. Don't visualize him as a man of grandiose proportions as the Babylonians visualized Marduk. Don't think of him as a force like electricity. Don't identify him with a mountain or the sky or any part of the universe or any point in time. He is spirit. Time and space have nothing to do with him. He indwells the universe and transcends the universe as your mind indwells and transcends your body. This is not so mysterious as it sounds.

"Grandfather," asked Dr. Lyman Abbott's small grandson,

"how can God be in Newburgh and Poughkeepsie at the same time?"

His grandfather touched him on the forehead. "Are you there?"

"Yes."

He touched him on the shoulder. "Are you there?"

"Yes."

He touched him on the knee. "Are you there?"

"Yes."

"That is how God can be in Newburgh and Poughkeepsie at the same time."

Where were you when on your last business trip you telephoned your home? In Chicago, where the call was made, or in your home where your family gathered around the receiver to hear your voice? Where are you when you are asleep? Have you ever noticed how different a person looks when asleep, all the animation and expression gone out of his face? Is it any wonder primitive peoples supposed that while a man slept his spirit left his body? Where are you now—in your hand or in your eyes or in your brain or off somewhere, thinking of something or someone a thousand miles away?

My mother was and is a strong influence in my life. Her influence was as strong when she lived in the old home in New Jersey and I lived in Cleveland as when we lived beneath the same roof, nor has it diminished as the years have passed since her death.

What am I getting at? This: God is spirit. You and I are spirit. Spirit with spirit can meet. Closer is he than breathing, nearer than hands and feet. He is here as though he were nowhere else. He is everywhere else as much as he is here. Ordinary measurements do not circumscribe him.

God Is Intelligent

Again we turn to Jesus, "Tell us more." He answers, "God is intelligent." We might have suspected this from a study of the universe: a universe which throughout its vast expanse reveals unity, order, design; a universe in which means are adapted to ends, effect follows from cause with unvarying regularity and faculty corresponds with environment as hand fits glove or key fits lock.

A thoughtful man says the most moving religious experience he ever had was not in a church but in a planetarium where a panorama of the universe was unrolled before his eyes. "That doesn't spell chance," he says, "it spells mind." A business-man I know has been studying atomic physics to find out what is going on. He says he does not see how anyone can study the structure of the atom without being convinced of an over-all intelligence. Said Albert Einstein not long before his death, "The scientist's religion takes the form of rapturous amazement at an intelligence compared with which all human thinking is insignificant."

When Jesus thinks of God's intelligence, he thinks of it in relation not to the universe but to the individual. According to Jesus, God's knowledge runs beyond our boldest imagination. We can number people, we cannot number birds. Some years ago the Audubon Society announced a census of the birds of the United States, but the birds would not stay still long enough to be counted. We can't number birds. Jesus says not a sparrow falls to the ground without God's knowledge.

There are one hundred seventy-five million people in the United States, over two billion in the world. How many billion have lived here, do you suppose, since human life first emerged on this planet perhaps half a million years ago? Is it possible with all this host that God knows you and me? Jesus says he knows us through and through. We don't need to blow a trumpet when we give alms. God sees our gift and the motive which prompts it. We don't need to shout when we pray. God is not deaf. He hears and will answer when we speak to him. He knows our sins that we hide so carefully from one another. He knows the strains and tensions of our lives, all we have tried to do and dreamed of doing:

> Thoughts hardly to be packed
> Into a narrow act,
> Fancies that broke through language
>   and escaped;
> All I could never be,
> All men ignored in me,
> This I was worth to God
> Whose wheel the pitcher shaped.

He is like a shepherd who calls his sheep by name, who misses from his flock even one lost lamb. The most degraded and abandoned member of the human family is not abandoned by him. He is spirit, the Father of our spirits. Ordinary measurements of number, time and space do not apply to him.

God Is Love

This brings us to Jesus' next statement which is bolder still: God not only knows us every one, he loves us every one. As St. Augustine put it, he so cares for each of us as if for him alone and so for all as if all were but one.

Men did not so believe in the long ages before Jesus came. The religions of antiquity—of Egypt, of Babylonia and Assyria, of Greece and Rome—never taught the love of their gods. The Jews believed that God loved them, his chosen people; but, with a few exceptions like the unknown genius who wrote Jonah, the unknown genius who wrote Isaiah 40 to 55, the unknown genius who wrote Malachi, they did not believe he loved the Egyptian who oppressed them, the Assyrian who conquered them, the Babylonian who deported them or the Roman whose eagles floated proudly over their holy city. There are elements of nobility in every religion, but the idea of God's love for every man—the last, the least, the lost—was brought into the world by Jesus.

One hesitates to use the word love, it has been so sentimentalized, even vulgarized. There is nothing sentimental about the love of God. As James Moffatt points out in his book, *Love in the New Testament,* the word translated "love" in the New Testament means not an emotion but a settled disposition of good will. It is like the devotion of a shepherd to his sheep; like the patience of a father whose headstrong son goes into

a far country and plays the fool, who longs for the boy's return yet respects his freedom; like the courage of the captain
of a sinking ship who stays on the bridge till the last passen-
ger is off; like that strange man hanging on a cross. Exhaust
all the analogies you can think of. The love of God is greater
than them all.

The man who wrote Psalm 103, declares Arthur John Gos-
sip, must have been a father. One day it came to him how
large a place his children filled in his life; how empty his life
would be without them; how naturally and without thinking
of it he spent himself for them; how, when one of them was
ill, he couldn't settle down to his work, couldn't get the hot
forehead and restless little hands out of his mind. Then it
came to him that God is like that, that "like as a father pities
his children, so the Lord pities those who fear him." Yes, says
Jesus, going a step further, those who fear him and those who
do not. The shabbiest prodigal of us all has a place in his heart
that no other can fill.

How do we know it is true? We don't in the same way
we know that a straight line is the shortest distance between
two points or that if we mix blue with yellow we'll get green.
But I remind you it is not the things you can prove that make
life worth living but the things you cannot prove. You cannot prove the love of your wife or the loyalty of your friend,
but you know it and build your life upon it. As an artist
like Rembrandt sees the beauty of light and shadow, as a com-
poser like Wagner hears the love-death music of Tristan, as a
lover feels the rapture of his love, as a seer knows the value

of his dream, so we know the love of God. We know it not by sight but by insight.

Always it will be an adventure—to be experienced, not proved. Always to cautious and skeptical souls there will be a touch of madness in it. Says Bishop Gore in his book, *Belief in God*, "To me the only difficult dogma of the church is the dogma that God is love." There are so many facts that seem to point in the other direction. Here is a young mother, smitten with an incurable disease. Her family stands helplessly by, watching her life slip away. Does God love her? Why doesn't he care for her? Why is this earth so dark with griefs and graves? It is hardly to be wondered that some find it easier to believe that the universe is in the grip of blind force rather than intelligent and loving will. A hurricane tears its way across the land, leaving death and desolation in its train. If God is love and in control, why?

It is only the unreflecting who are undisturbed by the sinister and ruthless aspects of nature. Thomas Huxley was an agnostic, the man who coined the word agnostic, but he had one of the keenest and most honest minds God ever put into a human skull. "I cannot see," he wrote Charles Kingsley, "one iota of evidence that the great unknown underlying the phenomena of the universe stands to us in the relation of father—loves and cares for us as Christianity asserts."

If we looked only where Huxley looked, we could not see either. If we were shut up to his facts, we should be shut up to his conclusion. There is just one fact that convinces me of the love of God, the fact of Jesus. Apart from him there is no

certain knowledge of it. It is significant that in the glowing
passage that brings the eighth chapter of Romans to a climax
and a close Paul does not speak of "the love of God" merely.
It is first "the love of Christ," then more fully "the love of
God which is in Christ." It is because God so loved that he
gave, because he spared not his own son, because on a cross
his love was nailed so high the proudest cannot fail to see it,
so low it is within the reach of all of us, that we dare to assert
that God is love and love is creation's final law.

God Is Power

Again we turn to Jesus asking, "Is there anything more?"
"Yes," he says, "he is a God of power." Though we have left
this till last, it was the first thing about God that man perceived. Primitive man discerned in it the howl of the wind
through the forest, the fierce raging of the storm. At first it
terrified him and he cringed before it. But as men learned to
know God better, they fortified and regaled themselves with
the thought of his power. They looked back across their
history at the wonders he had wrought. And he is the same
now, they said, "the God of Abraham, of Isaac, of Jacob and
our God." Or when the struggle seemed to be going against
them, they watched the slow procession of the stars across the
sky or listened to the surge and thunder of the surf upon the
shore: "O Lord, my God, thou art very great," they said, and
it comforted them.

How much greater is our thought of God's power as we
relate it to the universe science has disclosed. One night in an
observatory the astronomer pointed out the Cluster of Her-

cules, one of the nearer star clusters—you can see it with the naked eye. He told me it was 30,000 light years away, that the light I saw had been moving toward me at 186,000 miles a second since it left the Cluster of Hercules 30,000 years before. We can say with a fullness of meaning of which the prophet never dreamed, "Lift up your eyes on high and see: who created these? He who brings out their host by number, calling them all by name; by the greatness of his might and because he is strong in power, not one is missing."

But the dream on which his mind is set is that you and I and all men shall be sharers in his eternal purpose. He who holds the stars in their orbits, will he be thwarted here? No, he is equal to the task he has begun. He will see it through. He who began a good work in us is pledged to its completion. He has put high hopes in our hearts. He did not put them there to mock us. We can tackle the most stubborn problems in our own lives and in the world, knowing that he who sees the end from the beginning is on our side and at our side, and that therefore we cannot finally fail. He has invested in us too heavily to let us go.

This is what Jesus says is true about God: the infinite and eternal creator spirit to whom our spirits are kin, who knows us every one, loves us every one, who is strong enough to make his will prevail.

What's wrong with this picture? Only that in our low moods it seems too good to be true. But when we look from the picture to him who drew it and guarantees it, we feel instead it is so good it must be true.

What Sends Men to God

In Time of Stress

We rejoice that thou art one to whom we can come in every midnight hour. We want to enter more deeply into the life that is hid with thee, that it may not seem a strange and fearsome thing to turn to thee; but that we, like Jesus, may know whence to seek and where to obtain the reserves of power which enable men in every time of crisis, stress or seeming failure to find the peace of God that passes understanding; that we may pray as Jesus prayed in his midnight hour, "Father, into thy hands I commit my spirit." Amen.

WHAT SENDS MEN TO GOD

ANYONE WHO has ever had unexpected guests arrive late at night will sympathize with the luckless plight of the man in the little story recorded only by Luke and known as the Parable of the Friend at Midnight.

A flurried hostess extemporizes sleeping arrangements, gets out a supply of towels, then inquires of the belated arrivals if they have had supper. She knows that if they have any sense they will say yes. But the good sense of people who will drop in on one unannounced at odd hours cannot be counted on too strongly.

Sure enough, they allow the fact to become known that they have had nothing since lunch. The lady of the house hastens to a larder she knows is depleted, hoping she may at least find a jar of peaches and plenty of bread and butter to set before her famished guests or, failing that, be able to borrow from her next door neighbor.

Such is the situation in Jesus' story. The unexpected guest arrives at midnight. His host finds that his guest has missed his supper. He also finds himself out of bread. He goes next door and knocks, first gently, then with increasing vehemence. Presently a muffled voice asks what is wanted. He tells his story: awkward predicament at his house, a hungry guest and no bread.

The neighbor answers, "That's your problem! You have a nerve to come here. We're all in bed. The house is locked. We do not want to be disturbed. Will you kindly go away quietly so as not to wake the baby?"

The man has no intention of going away. He stays and continues his plea until his drowsy, disgruntled neighbor decides that the only course left to him, if he wants to get back to sleep, is to get up and give what is asked for. So he gropes his way to the kitchen, finds the bread box, opens the door just wide enough to slip the bread through, and the borrower returns home.

Persistence Wins

You perceive the obvious lesson of this homely tale: persistence wins. Every salesman knows this, knows the sale depends on which becomes exhausted first, his prospect's sales resistance or his perseverance. Every child knows it, knows that if he teases long enough for what he wants the odds are in favor of his getting it. He may first get one or two other things, intended to squelch him and impress on him that when his father says "no" he means "no"; but if the child doesn't let these slight setbacks deter him he'll finally wear his father down. We don't need to tell our children stories to teach them that if they are importunate enough they'll get what they go after. A three-year-old doesn't know the expression, "nuisance technique," but he is adept in the use of nuisance technique.

Persistence is a trait that Jesus admires. Several of his parables turn on it. Another, also unique to Luke, is the Parable of the Unjust Judge. This judge neither "feared God nor regarded man." Certainly he had no regard for a poor widow, a person of no importance. When she asked him to hear her case, he ignored her—gave her the brush-off.

But, like the man in the other story, she did not go away. When His Honor left home in the morning, there she was, waiting at the gate. She tailed him across town to the court house, calling at intervals, "When are you going to give me justice? When are you going to hear my case?" When he emerged from his chambers in the afternoon, she was waiting behind one of the columns on the courthouse porch, calling "When are you going to try my case?"

The lawyers and bailiffs began to twit him. "There's your lady friend waiting for you, Judge!" It wouldn't do. It imperiled his dignity, made him a laughing stock. So he said to himself, "Though I neither fear God nor regard man, yet because this widow bothers me I will vindicate her or she will wear me out."

In both stories Jesus is teaching the same thing: perseverance in prayer. Luke introduces the story of the Unjust Judge by saying, "He told them a parable to the end that they ought always to pray and not lose heart." He introduces the story of the Friend at Midnight with the statement that Jesus was praying in a certain place and when he ceased one of his disciples asked, "Lord, teach us to pray." He answered "When you pray, say"—then follows the Lukan form of the Lord's Prayer which is shorter than the familiar Matthean form. Most scholars think it is earlier, and that Matthew's is an expansion of it. Then comes the story of the Friend at Midnight.

In both parables Jesus uses the argument from contrast, the "how much more" argument. If a corrupt and callous judge will hear a woman who makes herself a nuisance to him, how much more will God listen to his children? If a churlish, boorish neighbor will finally respond to a man who makes himself a nuisance, how much more will persevering prayer bring a response from a God who is more ready to give than we to ask?

For, as Jesus goes on to say, if you human fathers know how to give good gifts to your children, how much more will the heavenly Father give to those who ask him. Therefore ask, seek, knock—the manner of speaking suggests perseverance—for everyone who asks receives, and he who seeks finds, and to him who knocks the door will open to reveal the riches of God's grace.

In Jesus' story the obstacles to be overcome were on the other side of the closed door—the selfishness and boorishness of the disobliging neighbor. In our approach to God the obstacles are on our side of the door—our laziness, inertia, indifference, lack of faith. Christ stands at the door of our lives and knocks. In his surpassing courtesy he does not push himself in where he isn't wanted; but if any one opens the door, he will come in.

Prayer is not an attempt to induce a reluctant deity to give us benefits he wants to withhold, as a child's teasing is an attempt to wear down his father's resistance. Prayer is a means of opening our lives to receive what God is always trying to bestow. Why do we need to pray? Because the doors and windows of the self tend to close tight, shutting out what God is ever seeking to impart. Through prayer the doors and windows are flung open again. The effect of persistent prayer is not a change wrought in God. It is a change wrought in us.

A Deeper Meaning

This lesson is plain, though we need to be reminded of it. Now look at the story more closely and see if it has a more subtle meaning. John Erskine says that in every great work of art there are two meanings: one that lies on the surface and is apparent to all; a second, deeper meaning—like the underlying irony of Greek tragedy—for those who have the wit to find it.

What is wrong with the story of the Friend at Midnight? This: neighbors do not act that way. To be sure, being awakened from a sound sleep puts a strain on a man's disposition, but not severe enough to warrant his losing his manners completely. More than once when emergencies have arisen in my domicile I have had to subject my neighbors' neighborliness to harder tests, and I have never been so treated.

Some days ago a caravan of five pilgrims descended on us. As soon as she heard of it, a neighbor put her guest room at our disposal. She didn't wait for us to ask. She made the offer. That's the kind of neighbors to have. That's the kind we've always had. We have our little differences. When their dog tears up our flower beds for a convenient place to bury his bones, it puts my wife's religion to the proof. But when we get in a hole they are there to help us out, and we are there to do the same for them.

There is nothing remarkable about that, you say. That is the point. It is the normal, natural thing to do. We like to minister to one another's necessities, relieve one another's distress. Nothing gives us more satisfaction than to be able to help someone out of a trying situation. More and more as we grow older we get more pleasure from helping others than from having them help us—the cynics would say because it ministers to our self-esteem, our sense of superiority, but it is not altogether that.

So this neighbor's refusal to help out in an emergency doesn't sound natural. I'm afraid his unwillingness was due to the fact that the man had not knocked at his door many times before. I suspect his failure to get up and grant the request was not due to laziness or stinginess but because he said to himself, "This fellow never comes over here unless he wants to borrow something or complain about the children. Otherwise he has no time for me. He holds himself aloof. I'll show him I can do the same." Not magnanimous, but understandable.

If there had been a well-worn path across the back yard through a hole in the hedge to his neighbor's back door, I can't believe his neighbor would have turned him down. "John! Bill speaking. Company landed in on us. Nothing in the house to eat." Before he had reached the end of the sentence, John would have had his bathrobe and slippers on and been paddling toward the kitchen.

What Jesus is trying to tell us is that this is how we treat God. We turn to him only when we are in trouble and need help. Because we are conscious of this, when we do turn to him we feel embarrassed and constrained. For in every good relationship the approach must come from both sides.

You see a man you think you would like to know. You make advances toward acquaintance and possible intimacy. But until he responds intimacy is impossible. His response is the prerequisite of friendship, just as our response is the pre-requisite of a deepening friendship with God. It is unfortunate and disconcerting if the first time we approach anyone we are trying to borrow something or asking a favor. He looks at us askance—or we are afraid he may.

Not so with a friend. We feel no hesitation in asking favors of him because we know what his response will be, know that anything he has is at our disposal, just as anything we have is at his. Indeed, we cannot help being a little glad when an emergency arises in our friend's life—not glad that he is in trouble but glad that we have a chance to show him how much he means to us.

One of the things we learn as we grow older is that we probably give our friends more happiness by letting them do kindnesses for us than by invariably trying to do kindnesses for them. I learned that first from a well-to-do woman in my first parish. She was what the supercilious would call a Mrs. Malaprop, lacking the advantages that education and breeding bestow, not quite to the manner born. She was always doing kindnesses to old people and poor people, yet she always found a way to let them do something for her. She knew the giving must not be all on one side—they would feel more self-respecting if they could make some return. It showed a fineness of feeling that no etiquette book can give. For any good relationship must be a two-way street. The approach must be from both sides.

Is not this what God wanted us to do when he put us here, a big family? To live together as the members of a real family live, helping the others and letting them help us, dependent on them and having them dependent on us, equally glad that we can lean on them and that they can lean on us. He never meant us to live as Robinson Crusoes, each on a self-made isle of isolation. "The most important thing in life," said Tolstoi, "is for man to unite with man. The worst thing is for men to go apart from one another."

This man in Jesus' story was, I suspect, a self-contained, self-sufficient fellow who prided himself on his independence, who liked to have it understood that he paid his way, that he'd not trouble others if they'd not trouble him, that he'd stay on his side of the fence if they'd stay on theirs. Then one night he found that he was not so self-sufficient as he supposed. Of course it had to come at the most inopportune time, as emergencies seem to do. Ordinarily this traveling friend would have been welcome. Why did he have to show up on this particular night when the larder was empty and so late that all the markets and even the delicatessen stores were closed? So he was forced by his need to swallow his pride, go next door and say in as ingratiating a tone as he can manage,

"Friend, lend me three loaves; for a friend of mine has arrived on a journey, and I have nothing to set before him."

How We Treat God

So we treat God. We Americans in particular have run the Emersonian doctrine of self-reliance into the ground. We act as though we had made ourselves, as though what we are were due to our own cleverness. If we felt any sense of dependence on God, we should regard it as a weakness or a sign that we were getting old. Dr. John Schindler in his widely read *How to Live 365 Days a Year,* in the chapter entitled "Basic Psychological Needs," says that religion helps people who have a sense of insecurity or incompetence. That is how many think of religion, as an opiate for insomniacs to be taken instead of a barbiturate; as a crutch for those who find the going hard, who can't quite make the grade.

Here are we, then, behind a door of our own making. And there is God. Always there, so that we always know where to find him. Always the same, so that however we change our attitude toward him we do not change him. Always loving us, always seeking our love in return, forever pressing on every soul that he has made, soliciting an invitation but not forcing his way in for in any true relationship the approach must come from both sides. Until his love awakens a response, he can only stand "outside the fast-closed door, in lowly patience waiting to pass the threshold o'er."

All around us we see people living without God, not vicious lives, just superficial lives—what Plato called "the unexamined life": a frivolous, unreflecting, butterfly existence, feeling no need of wisdom or strength beyond their own or any companionship beyond what their human friends can supply, yet getting along all right as long as the sun is shining. But how our self-confidence ebbs when the darkness closes in on us and midnight draws near. When we least want it and feel least prepared to meet it, the summons comes and we find too late that we have nothing in reserve and are undone unless we can draw on resources beyond our own. Then in our dire need we turn to God.

How unexpectedly emergencies come, how they try our souls when they come. Here is a woman, a happy wife and mother, returning from a vacation trip to learn that she has cancer. Here is a man in middle life offered an influential government post; to accept it means to relinquish an assured position. He wonders whether he has the stamina (the word he used was "guts") to stand up under the forces that will play on him, the pressures that will be brought to bear on him. Here are parents, who, having sacrificed to give their son every advantage, now see him going to ruin via gambling and drink. Here is a young man confronted by a stress of temptation so sudden and seductive it almost swept him off his feet. His hands trembled and his voice shook as he told me the story.

Well for them and all such if, when the emergency comes, there is a beaten path between them and God so that they do not have to grope their unaccustomed way to him with hesitant and stumbling feet, shamefaced because they have come so seldom before; but rather, the relationship is so close that in their hour of need they turn to him as naturally and instinctively as a hurt child runs to his mother's arms.

During the war a chaplain came to the cot of a dying Scotch soldier. Wanting to prepare him and not knowing how to begin, he said, "It's a time like this that makes a man think." "Padré," said the soldier, "a done ma thinkin' lang syne." He did not need to cast about desperately, frantically for something to hold to in that hour when all else was slipping from him. He had done his thinking long before.

When the emergency is upon us there is no time to prepare. We have to be prepared. The way to be prepared is to keep the path open between us and God so that when we need reserves of power we can draw on his inexhaustible supply.

If there is anything in our lives that is likely to interpose a barrier, a shut door between us and him—whether it be pride or resentment or uncleanness or whatever it may be—we had better get it out of our lives, the barrier down, the path well traveled before the midnight hour comes.

A Religion for the Midnight Hour

One final thought. The religion of Jesus is the religion for the midnight hour—the midnight of temptation, remorse, loneliness, sorrow, despair, however black and cheerless it may be. For the God whom Jesus called Father is not like the reluctant neighbor of his tale. If you want to see his picture of what God is like, turn to another of his stories, the story of the father and the reckless, headstrong boy.

During all the time the boy was in the far country, the father watched for him, prayed for him. As long as the boy stayed away there was nothing the father could do but wait and watch and pray. The approach has to come from both sides. But as soon as he saw him coming, he waited no longer. He ran to meet him, calling, "Welcome home, my son!"

Use or Lose

A Trust from Thee

Teach us to take life as a trust from thee and use it
it to the full. Save us from sloth, from self-
despising, from faintheartedness, from thinking
that because we cannot do some great thing we
can do nothing. May we so diligently employ
the talent thou hast entrusted to us as to win the
only rewards worth striving for: self-fulfillment,
a growing competence, a clean conscience, fidelity
to ourselves, our fellows and thee. Amen.

USE OR LOSE

"A MAN going on a journey called his servants together and put his property in their hands. To one he gave five talents, to another two, to another one, to each according to his ability." So begins one of the most thought-provoking of Jesus' parables. Thomas Carlyle saw in it the sharp thrust of truth: "This is the question of questions: what talent is born in you? how do you employ it?"

Though the parable was spoken in Aramaic and written in Greek, it has contributed two words to the English language; the noun *talent* and the adjective *talented*. These words may be used to describe aptitude in various fields but are most often used in describing artistic ability. A person is talented if he can sing, or play a musical instrument, or paint pictures.

It is too bad that we have so restricted their meanings. How about the person whose talent is imaginative sympathy, who can put himself in another's place and so knows what to do or say to give the other the help or comfort he needs? the person whose talent is to put everyone, no matter how timid or shy, at ease in a social gathering? the man whose talent is to run an office, a shop or a school as smoothly as a well-oiled machine and in such a way that the atmosphere is conducive to the growth of all concerned? the woman whose talent is to create a home where the color scheme is right, where the living room chairs are so arranged that you can have a conversation without raising your voice, a home which is a haven of peace and quiet joy? How about the ability to write a letter which conveys not only information but affection and encouragement?

We should extend the meaning so that no one can say, "I am not talented. I have no talent." That is always an alibi. The parable recognizes no such person. Said Charles Spurgeon, "God has no time to waste making nobodies."

We use the word talent in a derived sense. To the people to whom Jesus spoke it meant a sum of money—the largest money unit they knew—as much as a laborer could earn in twenty years. Goodspeed assumes it was worth $1000: "He gave one $5000, another $2000 and another $1000."* If a talent was the equivalent of $1000 when Goodspeed brought out his translation in 1939, it was worth $2000 in the present enfeebled estate of the once Almighty Dollar.

Jesus was not talking about pin money. The parable is sometimes construed as though the first man received a large sum, the second a medium sum, the third a small sum. No, even the third man received a substantial sum, a fortune in that land of extreme poverty where even the bare necessities came hard.

Dr. A. B. Bruce in *The Parabolic Teaching of Christ* (which, though published in 1882, is still a useful work) classifies the parables under three heads: parables of grace,

* The Complete Bible: An American Translation, The University of Chicago Press.

parables of judgment and theoretic parables. The three in the fifteenth chapter of Luke—the Lost Sheep, the Lost Coin, the Lost Son—are parables of grace. The Parable of the Cruel Tenant Farmers and that of the Marriage Feast of the King's Son are parables of judgment. Bruce classifies the Talents as a theoretic parable. We can see why. The Declaration of Independence asserts that all men are created equal. In this parable Jesus takes for granted that men are unequal and attributes their inequality to God. Which is right, Thomas Jefferson or Jesus? Is it possible to reconcile the two?

Then there is the arresting statement with which the parable ends: "To every one who has will more be given; from him who has not, even what he has will be taken away." This saying is found also in Luke at the end of the Parable of the Pounds* and in Mark as a detached saying, unrelated to any parable. It runs counter to the socialist trend which is strong in our day. In the parable the master gives "to each according to his ability." The socialist slogan is, "From each according to his ability, to each according to his need." Much recent legislation in European countries as well as our own has been based on that principle: take from the wealthy by graduated income and estate taxes, raise the level of the poor by various forms of subsidy or dole.

---

* Is the Talents, found only in Matthew, a variant form of the Pounds, found only in Luke, or are they twin parables like the Hidden Treasure and the Pearl of Great Price, similar but not identical? Scholars are disagreed. The Talents and the Pounds both begin with a man about to go on a journey entrusting his money to his servants. Both end with the saying, "To every one who has will more be given. . . ." But there are significant differences. Study them and see what you decide.

No one had more sympathy for the poor than Jesus. He said many things to comfort them, such as "Blessed are you poor, for yours is the kingdom of God."* He said harsh things about the rich, such as his comment on the rich young ruler, "How hard it will be for those who have riches to enter the kingdom of God! It is easier for a camel to go through the eye of a needle than for a rich man to enter the kingdom of God." Yet here he says, "To every one who has will more be given; from him who has not, even what he has will be taken away." Was this original with him or was he quoting a proverb that was going the rounds? Did he say or quote it with approval or simply as a statement of fact?

The deep cleavage that runs through society is between the "haves" and "have-nots." In spite of confiscatory taxes, those who have tend to get more. Money breeds money. Invested capital tends to grow. There are such things as stock splits, stock dividends, and expense accounts which are not subject to tax. Then again in the course of a long ministry, I observed how often young men of well-to-do families marry young women of well-to-do families, not because they are mercenary but because their families move in the same circle and they are thrown together.

Those who have tend to get more. Those who have not find it hard to hold on to what little they have. They live from hand to mouth, always trying to make ends meet. Some are thriftless and improvident. Some have no money sense. In-

---

* This is the Lukan form of the beatitude. Most scholars think it is the original form and that Matthew has weakened it, "Blessed are the poor in spirit. . . ."

stead of receiving interest on their investments, they are constantly paying interest on their debts. There are thousands of young families who are budgeted to the last dollar to meet the payments on their homes, their cars, their television sets, their appliances. If an unbudgeted expense—a heavy repair bill or an unplanned baby—hits them, they are sunk. As the old song says, "the rich get richer and the poor get poorer." Where is the justice of it?

Though Bruce classifies the Talents as a theoretic parable, it can also be classed as a parable of judgment, for the master on his return passes judgment on his servants—on two a favorable judgment, on the third an adverse and severe judgment. Matthew (whose gospel is highly schematized) puts it between two other parables of judgment, the Wise and Foolish Bridesmaids and the Separation of the Sheep from the Goats. These three parables make up the twenty-fifth chapter of Matthew. He puts them at the very end of Jesus' teaching ministry, then goes on at once to the last crowded week of Jesus' life.

Here is another consideration. When I taught New Testament to college students, I told them that Jesus' parables could not be pressed at every point, that he observed the first law of attention—one idea at a time, that in each parable he was trying to teach a single truth. On a test I asked the class to name ten parables and tell in a sentence what Jesus was trying to teach.

Does that principle hold true of the Parable of the Talents? There are several ideas that lie right on the surface. When scholars probe into it, they find others still. For ex-

ample, some think that when Jesus pictured the man who
buried his talent, he had in mind the devout Jew who hugged
his religion—the Torah, the Law—to himself but had no interest in projecting it or sharing it with others; that Jesus was
animadverting upon the monopolistic, exclusive tendency in
religion which survives in some quarters among his own followers. Some say that the parable is eschatological; that is,
pertaining to the last things, the end of the age and the judgment, the second advent when Jesus will return and get an
accounting from his servants and on the basis of it reward or
punish them.

It may be. But I suspect that commentators read too much
into the parables, read into them their own preconceived
ideas, just as Shakespearean scholars read into Shakespeare
ideas that were never in his mind. I can never get away from
the fact that Jesus was not lecturing to university graduates,
he was talking to plain folk. It was the common people, we
are told, who heard him gladly. He was not trying to mys-
tify them.* He was trying to state eternal truth so simply
and clearly that they could take it in. Let us take the parable
at its face value and see what it has to say.

Inequality of Endowment

Look first at this idea of inequality of endowment. Note
that the men in the story did not earn the talents. They were
given them by their master—by implication, God. This is

* One of his reporters thought that he was—see Mark 4:11, 12 and paral-
lels—but I am sure that he misunderstood Jesus' intention.

in line with modern thought. The given factor, what we are born with, the result of a certain combination of genes, is more important in determining our ability than anything we acquire after we are born. To educate means to educe, to draw out. Many a commencement speaker has harped on this theme. Education can draw out what is there. It cannot put in what is not there. Those of us who hold to the religious view of life believe that this native endowment comes not by happy accident nor from the good fairies who waved their magic wands over our cradle: it is the gift of God.

But we are not endowed equally. Talents are not evenly distributed. Those who have more to begin with find it easier to increase what they have. To put it bluntly, those who have, get. Whether or not it is fair, there is no doubt that it is so.

Nothing impressed me more when I was teaching than the wide range of ability in my classes. Here was a group of young men and women, all of them graduates of an approved high school. Most of them had taken the College Entrance Board tests. All of them had been screened by the admissions office. You would suppose they would be a fairly homogenous group. On the last Old Testament final I gave, the low grade was 28, the high 98; on the last New Testament final, the low was 22, the high 97.

You will say rightly that this result was due not only to difference in intelligence but to difference in effort. One student applies himself, does hard, consistent work. His roommate dawdles. He may sit at a desk with an open book before him but no transfer takes place. Yet here again why has one something inside him which impels him to do his best, while another lacks initiative, drive, the will to do, the ability to stick at a thing, to organize his time, to "energize at his maximum," as William James put it?

The student with an I.Q. of 140 finds lessons come easy. He excels at them. We tend to like to do what we excel at. So he studies the more diligently. Everything he learns makes it easier for him to learn more. The boy in the next seat finds it all he can do to keep his head above water. His only incentive is the negative one of avoiding failure.

(Do not think me an intellectual snob. A study of Harvard graduates—a candidate for a Ph.D. made this the subject of his thesis—indicates that there is a direct correlation between scholastic achievement and success in later life. Yet sometimes a C student is a more attractive, trustworthy person and becomes a more useful member of society than his brilliant classmate. So far as I can see, there is no direct correlation between intelligence and happiness or between intelligence and moral reliability. A prison warden boasted to me that among his charges were men capable of teaching every subject in a college curriculum, including Bible. I simply point out the wide variation in mental equipment.)

Endowment is unequal. Those who have, get. The principle holds true of popularity. One finds it easy to draw people to him. He is outgoing, a natural leader. Wherever he sits is the head of the table. Another is shy, introverted, awkward in his contacts with people. He would like to have friends but does not know how to make them.

The principle holds true in business and the professions.

One food market has a growing volume as one satisfied customer tells another. Its turnover is so rapid that its stock is always fresh. One doctor's practice grows till he has more patients than he can take care of. One lawyer has to turn clients away. The writer of a successful book finds a readier sale for the next. Success breeds success.

Everywhere we see the principle at work. As Luke quotes Jesus in another connection,* "Every one to whom much is given, of him will much be required; and of him to whom men commit much they will demand the more." Of the able, vigorous, up-and-coming man, the community expects more than it does of the mediocrity, the failure. Heavier responsibilities are laid upon him. But this too is an incentive. We tend to measure up to what people expect of us.

Its Justification

This inequality of endowment is hard for us to understand and accept. When we were in grade school we memorized the heightened words of the Declaration already alluded to: "We hold these truths to be self-evident, that all men are created equal . . ." Lincoln had them in mind as he began his Gettysburg Address: "Four score and seven years ago our fathers brought forth on this continent a new nation . . . dedicated to the proposition that all men are created equal." Jesus in this parable holds it to be self-evident that men are created unequal. He does not argue it. He assumes it.

* In the Parable of the Unfaithful Steward, Luke 12:48.

We Americans believe passionately in democracy. Many equate democracy with equalitarianism, resent any implication that one man is better than another. In the old days when a stagecoach became mired the driver would call, "First class passengers, keep your seats. Second class passengers, get out and walk. Third class passengers, get out and push." Knowing the temper of the American people, my guess is that when the emergency arose all the able-bodied male passengers realized that they were on an equal footing—an equally slippery footing; all got out and pushed. A recent best seller, Walter Lord's *A Night to Remember*, gives a thrilling account of the sinking of the *Titanic*. I have a vivid memory of that disaster. Not even the repeated disregard of iceberg warnings caused more resentment than that first class passengers were given first chance to get into the life boats, steerage passengers last. We Americans don't go for that.

I yield to no one in my admiration for the signers of the Declaration, the founding fathers of our nation. But they were under the influence of certain rhetoricians masquerading as philosophers—Voltaire, Rousseau, Thomas Paine. Moreover, they were in protest against the Old World idea that men are divided into patrician and plebeian, lord and serf, master and man.

Jesus looked at men with clearer eyes. He did not say that all are created equal, for this is obviously not so. He said that all are equally dear to God, that each has his place in God's love that no other can fill. As the implications of his teaching become plain, we see with increasing clearness that, so far as we can insure it, all should have equal opportunity.

We Americans are convinced and have followed through

on our conviction that it is not fair that one should have a good education because of the fortunate circumstances into which he was born, while another is deprived of it. We have replaced the old aristocratic conception of education by the democratic. From kindergarten to university, we have opened the avenues of opportunity to all. This is the glory of democracy. This is why, in spite of its shortcomings, we believe in it. More than any other social system yet devised, it has brought equality of opportunity.

But equality of opportunity is one thing, equality of endowment is another. This no government, no educational system can bestow. One enters life equipped with a robust body, another with a frail, perhaps deformed body which handicaps him all his days. One has a high intelligence, which means that learning comes easily; another a low intelligence, which means that learning comes hard. One girl has a pretty face and a merry line and in consequence plenty of male attention. Another has not. If we had been consulted as to our physical and mental make-up, some of us would have had a few changes to suggest. We were not. We have to take the hand that is dealt us and play it as well as we can.

In the parable this inequality is attributed to God. "It isn't fair," you say, "If I were God I'd give all men an even chance." Yet when we look at life with eyes that are envy-free, we know that it is richer because of this inequality. Better that poetic ability be concentrated in a Milton, musical ability in a Beethoven, the ability to paint in a Raphael, and the rest of us cultivate the art of appreciation, than that there be a dead level, a "socialization" of artistic ability with resultant mediocrity. Better that Pasteur have five talents in science, Edison and Kettering in invention, and that we all benefit from their labors as we do.

Moreover, as life is organized, there are many necessary tasks which require only one talent. But if that talent is not faithfully used, the whole organization bogs down. The crew is no more dependent on the captain than the captain on the crew. The man on the assembly line is no more dependent on the production manager than the manager is on him.

The man who buried his talent was not a scoundrel. He did not make off with his master's money and squander it in riotous living. He simply lacked the imagination to see that his talent was needed. He undervalued himself and the service he could render. He failed to realize that money is a medium of exchange and that when it is withdrawn from circulation it no longer fulfills the purpose for which it was made.

In Chartres Cathedral, Gothic architecture—"the noblest tribute ever paid by a religion to its god"—comes to its zenith. It was a community project. Every one contributed what he could. The men who gave so many days' work to quarry the stone and move it to the site were as indispensable as those whose artistry wrought the soaring spires, the many-splendored windows, the deftly carved organ rail. As Browning sings in *Pippa Passes*, "All service ranks the same with God: there is no last nor first."

Most of the world's work, most of the vast aggregate of kindness is done by ordinary people. Some of the most useful men I know are men of modest endowment who more than compensate for their limited ability by the wholeheartedness of their effort and the fineness of their spirit.

The trouble with most of us, if we are honest enough to admit it, is not that we lack intelligence and ability enough to make a good contribution but that we do not make full use of what we have. As William James says, we suffer from a tendency to minimum effort. We never use one per cent of the brain cells given us to think with and through. We seldom use a tithe of the energy at our disposal. We are not reservoirs of energy in danger of running dry. We are channels through which a stream of energy flows.

We wish we had larger ability. Are we living up to what we have? We were made to do something. Hands, feet, brain, the power to crystallize thought into action: these were not given us as ornaments, they were given us to use. God expects no more from us than our best—not an ideal best, our best. If we fail to give it, we are wicked and slothful servants, like the sluggard in Jesus' tale.

The Reward of Fidelity

Men are judged not by what they have but by how effectively they use it. Note that inequality of endowment does not mean inequality of treatment. To the man whose five talents earned five more his master says, "Well done, good and faithful servant. You have been faithful over a little. I will set you over much. Enter into my joy." When the second man whose lesser endowment has earned a lesser increment makes his report, he receives the same hearty commendation, not a word changed.

This master does not expect the impossible. Sharp as he

seems in looking after his interest, he has not fallen into the vulgarity of rating his servants by the amount of money they bring to his coffers. He rates them by the diligence and devotion they bring to his service. If the third man had brought back his single talent with its hard earned surplus, he would have received the same commendation given the other two. He is condemned, not because he has only one talent, but because he is too lazy or too timid to put it to use. It was not failure but the prospect of failure that daunted him. As Ananias is the patron saint of liars, he is the patron saint of slackers and shirks.

The plain teaching of the parable is that equal fidelity in the use of unequal opportunity is equally rewarded. The decisive factor is not how many talents we have, but how well we employ what we have. The reward of fidelity is increased capacity. The man who makes good on a modest assignment thereby fits himself for a larger one. Every time we decline an opportunity that has our name on it, we make ourselves less fit, less inclined to respond to the next.

According to the old bromide, we get out of life as much as we put in. In point of fact, we get out far more than we put in. There is an unearned increment. But just as the farmer has to plow and plant his fields before he can avail himself of the forces of the universe—the sun, the rain, the fertility of the soil—so we have to put something in!

The Penalty of Sloth

This brings us to the negative aspect, the penalty of sloth, the tragedy of disuse: "from him who has not, even what he has will be taken away." This is obvious too. The used muscle grows stronger; the unused muscle grows flabby and soft. The unused member atrophies, which is why man has only the rudiment of a tail, why fish in the darkness of Mammoth Cave have only sockets where once were eyes. The man who does not use his mind will in time have none to use.

People lament that they have poor and unreliable memories. How much do you exercise your memory? When I taught Bible I required my students to learn about twenty dates from 1290 B.C., the approximate date of the Exodus, to Bar Kokba's revolt, 132-135 A.D., which marked the end of the Jewish state till it was re-established in 1948. These dates provide a framework for the history and enable the student to locate the significant events, ideas and personalities in their correct period and sequence. Some of my students complained bitterly, insisted that they could not possibly learn twenty dates. I said to them, "Some of you are going on to law or medical school. What I ask of you is child's play compared with what will be expected of you there. For example, there are more than two hundred bones in the human body. A doctor cannot know most of them. He has to know all of them, where they are and what they are for."

Memory is a phase of attention. It is astonishing how it can be developed. The same is true of reasoning, reflection, judgment, imagination and thinking in general. Says Dean George R. Harrison of Massachusetts Institute of Technology in an article entitled "How the Brain Works," "The circuits of the mind improve with use and exercise. Thinking brings an increased blood supply and more nourishment to the cells involved." If there is a law of diminishing returns, there is also a law of increasing returns.

Use or lose! The principle holds true all along the line. I stress it because the characteristic sins of respectable people are sins of omission.

> I never cut my neighbor's throat;
>   My neighbor's gold I never stole;
> I never spoiled his house and land;
>   But God have mercy on my soul!
>
> For I am haunted night and day
>   By all the deeds I have not done;
> O unattempted loveliness!
>   O costly valor never won!*

God Has Invested In You

Here is the sum of the matter. Life is a trust committed to us by God who wants us to make the most of ourselves and the best of ourselves. This is the most fruitful, the most invigorating way of looking at life. Make it a part of your working philosophy as it has long been a part of mine.

One of the strongest incentives I have had is that my parents invested in me. I was the oldest of four children. It took careful planning on my father's part to give me the rich opportunities I had. If he had had a grain of selfishness in his make-up, he would never have done for his children what he did. My first and best teacher in religion was my mother.

* Marguerite Wilkinson

Most of my working theology, as distinguished from what I
have read in books, I learned from her. The time lengthens
since they passed beyond my sight but the incentive remains.
I should hate to admit to myself that I was an investment
that turned sour.

But the prior investment, the major investment was God's.
Whatever talent I have he gave me and gave me to use. I
should hate to wash out on him.

God has invested in you. Say it to yourself in the hour of
your success when, like Little Jack Horner, you are tempted
to say, "What a great boy am I!" Say rather, "God has invested in me." Repeat it to yourself when you are feeling low,
in one of the "what good am I? what's the use? what's it all
about?" moods that now and again beset us: "God has invested in me."

Ability sets the limit to achievement. Motivation determines how close to that limit we come. The highest motive
for the use of our talents is gratitude to him who gave them
to us.

I mentioned a test in which I asked a class to list ten parables and tell in a sentence what each was intended to teach.
A girl gave me this on the Talents:

> What we are is God's gift to us;
> what we become is our gift to him.

Many Called, Few Chosen

Grace to Accept

Lord Jesus, who didst liken the kingdom of God
    to a wedding feast given by a king,
  give us grace to accept the king's invitation
    with grateful and astonished joy,
  insight to perceive that privilege carries with it
    responsibility, and
  willingness to prove worthy of the opportunity
    that is ours.
In this tumultuous time in which our lives are set,
  empower us to think and will and do
  what they must think and will and do
  who take this invitation seriously. Amen.

MANY CALLED, FEW CHOSEN

"MANY ARE CALLED but few are chosen." This is one of Jesus' hard sayings. It has puzzled many and offended not a few. It sounds harsh on the gracious lips of him who said, "Come to me, all who labor and are heavy laden," and "Him who comes to me I will not cast out." But it does not do to dismiss a saying because it is difficult. Rather we must dig down into it till we find what it means. Let us look first at the parable which leads up to it, the little-known Parable of the Wedding Feast of the King's Son or the Slighted Invitation. Perhaps it will give us a clue.

As we noted in the last chapter, Dr. A. B. Bruce in his *Parabolic Teaching of Christ* classifies the parables under three heads: theoretic parables such as the Friend at Midnight and the Talents (studied in the two preceding chapters), parables of grace such as the Prodigal (studied in the next chapter), and parables of judgment such as this.

"They Made Light of It"

It is a highly improbable story. A certain king gives a marriage feast for his son and sends servants to call those who had been invited. This was in line with Oriental custom. Invitations were issued well in advance. When the time came, servants were sent to remind the guests. But when the servants called them, they would not come.

Then the king sent other servants to commend the dinner to them, to tell them that the food was prepared, the tables were set, and to beseech them to come. But they made light of it. They not only spurned his hospitality, they refused to take his invitation seriously. Some were indifferent, preoccupied with their own affairs, one with his farm, another with his business. Some were actively hostile. They laid hold of the king's servants, treated them shamefully and killed them.

When this was reported to the king he was angry, as he had good cause to be. He sent his troops to destroy those murderers and burn their city. Then he said to his servants, "The wedding is ready but those invited were not worthy. Go out into the streets and invite everybody you can find." There was a plentiful response to this sweeping invitation. When the king came into the banquet hall it was filled with guests.

This, I repeat, is an unlikely story. A wedding is a gala occasion. When we are invited to one we are not reluctant to attend. We are pleased and flattered that anyone thinks enough of us to include us in this solemn, joyous event in the family life. We send as good a present as we can afford, wrapped in tissue paper and white ribbon. When the appointed day arrives we put on our best clothes and best manners and sally forth.

How much more impressed we would be, how eager to do the right thing, if the invitation came from some one of prominence, to be admitted to whose circle we regarded as a high honor. We can hardly imagine a king having to send a second time to those he had invited, extolling the quality of the entertainment provided and begging them to come. We can scarcely conceive of royalty humbling itself to say, "My oxen and fat calves are killed. Everything is ready. I implore you to come."

But the unlikelihood of the story gives it force both for Jesus' day and ours. The Jews regarded themselves as a religious aristocracy. For centuries they had been taught that they were God's chosen people. From the prophets they had received intimation of the coming day of the Lord. Then they heard from John the Baptist, from Jesus and his apostles that the day was at hand. But they held aloof. Some were indifferent, preoccupied. Some were hostile to the point that they murdered John the Baptist* and—as Jesus foresaw, for this parable was spoken in his last week—him. He may also have been warning his disciples of the fate that awaited them.

Jesus' teaching here is the same as in the parable which immediately precedes this, the Parable of the Wicked Husbandmen (tenant farmers, we would call them) who abused the servants (meaning the prophets) whom the owner of the vineyard sent to them. When he finally sent his son saying, "They will respect my son," they seized and killed him (Jesus' prophecy of his own death).

The vengeance of the outraged king in the parable we are

---

* Herod Antipas, who beheaded John the Baptist at the instigation of Herodias and Salome, was not a Jew by blood but was ruler of Galilee. It was to him that Pilate, trying to evade responsibility, sent Jesus when he found that he was a Galilean. Herod treated Jesus with contempt and sent him back to Pilate. So Luke 23:6-12.

studying—"he destroyed those murderers and burned their city"—evidently alludes to the destruction of Jerusalem by the Romans under Titus in the year 70. Whether Jesus actually used these words or they were attributed to him after the event, scholars are disagreed. To the writer of Matthew (published about 85) the destruction of Jerusalem was not an accident of history but God's retribution for its rejection of Jesus.

There is no doubt but that Jesus at first conceived his mission as to his own nation. They were the ones to whom God's invitation was first to come. In the tenth chapter of Matthew we read that when he sent forth the Twelve he charged them not to go among the gentiles or the Samaritans "but to the lost sheep of the house of Israel." In the fifteenth chapter of Matthew, in the incident of the Syrophoenician woman who besought his help for her stricken daughter, we are told that at first he did not answer her, saying to his disciples in explanation, "I was sent only to the lost sheep of the house of Israel." Even when she came and knelt before him he said, "It is not fair to take the children's bread and throw it to the dogs." "But," persisted the woman, "even the dogs eat the crumbs which fall from their masters' table." Then Jesus, moved not only by her quick wit but by his own quick sympathy, said, "Woman, great is your faith," and granted her request. Mark correctly interprets this incident as a turning point in Jesus' ministry when it was borne in upon him that the divine invitation which his own people had rejected must be freely offered to mankind.

In this parable we find that conviction fully developed. When the original guests scorned the invitation, the king sent his servants "to the partings of the highways" (a meta-phor for the gentile world) to invite all they could find. We are left to imagine the hilarious joy of the motley throng who unexpectedly find themselves in the lighted room around the well-filled tables in the presence of the king. The best com-mentary on this is the Book of the Acts where we read of the amazing success of the gentile mission, how Christ's servants spread the invitation through the Graeco-Roman world, how the stone that the builders rejected became the head of the corner.

So much for the bearing of the story on Jesus' time. Now for our own. There are those whom the king has invited by all the winsome solicitations of a Christian home, a Christian ancestry, a Christian heritage. But they make light of it and go their way. Their lives are full. They feel no need of what Christ offers. The church does not confront active hostility today save in lands where the religious situation is involved in the political situation. But it is handicapped, its power dimin-ished, its service curtailed by the chilling indifference of those whom it has a right to expect to be its loyal friends.

I think of one, typical of many. He had godly parents who reared him in "the nurture and admonition of the Lord." His fine character is in part at least a bequest from them. He had Sunday school teachers who helped train his conscience and ground him in principles of conduct which he has never aban-doned. He spent four years at a college founded by the church, equipped and endowed by the gifts of Christian peo-ple. I visited him once when he was recovering from an oper-ation in a hospital built and maintained by Christian people.

When children came, he brought them to the church to be dedicated to God in the beautiful rite of baptism, claiming for them a place in his love and grace, vowing to rear them by precept and example in Christian truth and duty. But his days are absorbed by his profession in which he is climbing fast. His evenings are filled with social engagements, for he is a charming fellow with a host of friends. The faith of his fathers is ignored.

He picked me up one day as I was waiting for a bus. As he set me down at my destination he smiled a little sheepishly and said, "So long, dominie, see you in church." I must have looked skeptical for he continued, "Some Sunday I'm going to surprise you." He is a smart man but not smart enough to perceive that to whom much is given, of him something may justly be required. Still Christ comes to his own and his own receive him not. Still he calls but they make light of it and go their ways.

"That My House May Be Filled"

Now look at the next point in the story. Its meaning is equally clear. When those who had been called would not come, the king bade his servants go out into the streets and invite all they found. In the similar Parable of the Great Banquet—found only in Luke—after all who had been invited asked to be excused, the master says to his servant, "Go out to the highways and hedges and constrain people to come in that my house may be filled." This is what the Master is saying to us. This is our business, to constrain people to come in that his house may be filled. This is where we fall down. There are devoted Christians who do everything but this. They come to church themselves, give liberally to its support, help it in many ways—but not in this all-important way. Someone with a flair for statistics has computed that it takes thirty Protestants a year to bring one new member into the church. Search your memory. How many have you brought in the past year, the past five years, all the years since you yourself took the vows of discipleship?

People do not come to church because required by the civil law as they were in colonial New England or because not to do so would subject them to criticism and perhaps ostracism. I am glad that those pressures have been removed. People do not come to church to make social contacts or improve their social status. They can do that more advantageously at the country club or even the parent-teacher association. I am glad that people no longer come to church because it is fashionable—except on Easter. People do not come to church for intellectual stimulus as they did in a day when books and libraries were scarce and the minister and the schoolmaster the only university-trained men in the community. They need not in a day when every town has a public library, every home a radio and television set, and everyone who wants an education can get it. There is but one force strong enough to bring men today: the love of Christ as revealed in his friends. "Go out into the highways and constrain people to come in," said Jesus. "The love of Christ constrains us," said Paul as he went out into the highways in obedience to Christ's behest. To give the invitation, to bring men in that the Lord's house may be filled: that is our business, as Jesus in this parable makes plain.

"Who Had Not on a Wedding Garment"

This brings us to the last incident of the parable. The servants invited all whom they saw, and many responded. When the king came in to greet them, he saw a man who was not wearing a wedding garment. This does not seem a serious offense to us for American men are not punctilious in the matter of attire. One of the readiest ways of honoring an occasion is to be appropriately and decorously clad. If you had an audience with the President or were to appear before the Supreme Court, you would not go in sports clothes and a fancy tie as though you were off to the races; you would find out what was called for and you would wear it. But in general American males are an informal lot. We like slouch hats. We don't like top hats.

Other times, other manners. Oriental etiquette in the matter of clothes was strict. For a man to appear at a wedding banquet without the garment custom prescribed was as much a breach as for a man now to pass a woman of his acquaintance on the street without lifting his hat. It was a mark of boorishness, of discourtesy, of lack of breeding or of regard for one's host.

This man said to himself, "Promiscuous affair. No one of any consequence will be there—just Tom, Dick and Harry. I'll not bother to change. I'll go just as I am." He was willing to partake of the feast, accept the hospitality provided;

unwilling to go to the trouble of making himself fit to remain, to do the one thing in his power to show his appreciation. Others had made light of the invitation and stayed away. He made light of it and came.

When the king saw him he asked, "Friend, why did you come here without being properly dressed?" The man was speechless. He had nothing to say. Up to this time his attitude had been jaunty and nonchalant as though he were conferring a favor on the party by being there at all. Suddenly he found himself in the presence of the king. He was filled with confusion and shame.

Then the king said to his servants, "Bind him hand and foot and cast him into the outer darkness: there men weep and gnash their teeth." It seems a severe penalty for so slight an offense. One would think it enough for him to have been ejected from the company to which he had shown himself not fit to belong. Maybe the king's temper, already sorely tried, got the better of him and he gave way to one of the sudden fits of anger in which Oriental monarchs indulged, issuing the most ruthless orders on slight provocation.

But what Jesus is teaching here is that heedlessness and thoughtlessness are not laughing matters. They may lead to fatal consequence. There are two ways of sinning against grace. One is brusquely to reject it as did those who refused the king's invitation. The other is to accept it in a flippant, careless spirit, making no attempt to prove worthy of it, as do those of whom this churlish fellow was the type.

We can go only where we fit ourselves to go. We can enjoy only the company with which we fit ourselves to mingle.

The boor does not feel at home with cultivated people, nor the ignoramus with scholars, nor the miser among philanthropists. We read of Judas that "he went to his own place." As water seeks its own level, so every man goes to his own place, the place to which he fits himself to go. It was not by chance that Jesus chose Peter, James and John to accompany him to the Mount of Transfiguration. They were the ones who had the spiritual preparedness to see what was there disclosed.

If you want Jesus' own commentary on this, turn to the twenty-fifth chapter of Matthew, the sublime and awful scene where the Son of Man is depicted as setting some on his right hand and some on his left. It is his vivid way of saying that only those fit to live eternally can inherit eternal life.

"Many Are Called but Few Are Chosen"

Now we are ready for the cryptic, epigrammatic statement with which the story ends, "Many are called but few are chosen." We noted at the beginning that it sounds harsh and at variance with Jesus' hopeful view of human possibilities, but in the light of this parable we see why it is so.

Have you noticed how many of Jesus' parables turn on fitness? For example, the Parable of the Drag Net. The net was cast into the sea and every kind of fish was gathered into it. But when it was filled the fishermen sat down on the beach, put the fish that were fit to eat into containers and threw the rest away. The parables of the Wise and Foolish Builders and the Wheat and Tares turn on the same question—the question of fitness.

So does the other wedding parable, the Parable of the

Bridesmaids. The foolish five were shut out from the marriage feast because they had not prepared themselves to meet the emergency which arose when the bridegroom was detained. They did nothing wicked. They did not throw stones at the wedding procession, nor insult the bride, nor steal the presents. They simply failed to fit themselves to discharge the one duty entrusted to them. Their friend had asked them to be light-bearers, but when the hour struck their lamps were dark for lack of oil.

Does not Jesus here put his unerring finger on the thing that most deeply differentiates men from one another? Some make themselves adequate to meet life's demands. Others meet them in a careless, flippant way. Young man, young woman, let this sink down into your mind: life's highest duty, life's highest satisfaction is found in making one's self fit to meet life's demands as they come.

One day two ardent, ambitious, headstrong youths came to Jesus with a request: "Grant that we may sit, one on your right, the other on your left, in your glory." Jesus answered, "That distinction is not mine to confer. It is for those for whom it has been prepared. Are you able to drink the cup that I drink, to be baptized with the baptism I am baptized with?" Are you able? Not often in the course of a life time is one brought face to face with such a challenge. When it comes it behooves us to be ready for it; to answer with James and John, "We are able;" then give the rest of our lives to make it good.

Here is another of Jesus' hard sayings: "Enter by the narrow gate. For the gate is wide and the way is easy that leads to destruction and those who enter by it are many. For the gate is narrow and the way is hard that leads to life and those who find it are few." It is a principle which Jesus states again and again and of which a thousand illustrations can be found: many called, few chosen.

We see the principle at work in the field of education. It is one of the glories of our country that from kindergarten to university the avenues of education are open. Up to a certain age the state compels children to go to school and their parents to send them on the theory that a democracy requires a literate electorate. After that, be they rich or poor, if they have the requisite health and ambition they can go on to obtain the finest education the land affords. This broadening of educational opportunity is one of the striking phenomena of our time.

In 1870 there were 80,000 students in our high schools. In 1950 there were 8,000,000. While the population of the country increased fourfold (from 38,558,000 to 150,697,-000), the high school enrollment increased a hundredfold. Despite the barrage of criticism leveled at our high schools—strong in driver training, home economics, athletics and extracurricular activities; weak in mathematics, foreign languages and the physical sciences—the scholastic standard of the best high schools is steadily rising. In some subjects their students do work of college grade.

A Princeton senior wrote home that on the morning after the prom certain seniors took their girls to a seminar in economics so that Princeton became for a day coeducational. The professor asked a question of a member of the class who unfortunately had fallen asleep, worn out from his exertion the night before, whereupon his girl answered for him.

"An excellent answer," said the professor, "where did you learn that?"

"In high school," said the girl.

The flocking of the youth of America to its colleges is one of the major mass movements of history. In 1892, the year I was born, there were 74,000 students in our colleges. Not till 1898 did the number reach 100,000. In 1910, the year I entered college, it had risen to 183,000. Now it is 3,500,000. It is predicted that—due to the high birth rate during the war and immediate postwar years—it will be 4,500,000 by 1965. College administrators are wondering how their already taxed facilities for housing and instruction can take care of them.

This tidal wave of students has profoundly modified the character of the higher learning. The old aristocratic conception and the classic tradition based upon it—inherited from Oxford and Cambridge—had been long dying. The GI Bill of Rights gave them their death blow. A college education, even an Ivy League college education, no longer has any prestige value. It has become an item in the American standard of living.

But alas! only a small percent of these multitudes become educated, only a fraction seriously try to be numbered among the intellectually competent. A college president was showing a visitor over the campus. "About how many students have you?" asked the visitor. "About one in a hundred," was the reply.

The road to the summit is open but it is narrow and steep. Many fall by the wayside or are lured into bypaths on either hand. Ours is a day of short cuts and labor saving devices but as true now as it was when Euclid said it, there is no royal road to learning. It comes only to those who "scorn delights and live laborious days." Many have no desire to scorn delights and live laborious days, never feel at home in the precincts of learning, perceiving neither the austerity of its demands nor the graciousness of its rewards. They are willing to attend the rich feast of educational privilege but reluctant to do it honor.

A study of this parable might well be made a college entrance requirement; and if somewhere in the diploma could be woven in the sentence, "Many are called but few are chosen" (perhaps in its Latin form to make it more impressive, "Multi enim vocati sunt, pauci vero electi"), it might have a chastening effect on the hosts in cap and gown who move in stately processionals across our campuses each June.

What is true of education is true in every realm: many called, few chosen. Gideon's army is typical: thirty-two thousand were called, but after a series of elimination tests by which their fitness was tried, three hundred were chosen. In this searching parable Jesus shows how and why the principle holds in the highest realm of all. The invitation is freely given, but many ignore it. Of those who accept it, many fail to fit themselves for "the life which is life indeed."

Here is the explanation. The calling is of God. But the choice rests with you.

He Came to Himself

The Fullness of a Father's Love

We thank thee that as soon as a prodigal comes to himself
   all the forces of heaven are released to find and to restore;
   that when he says, "I will arise and go to my father,"
   he finds awaiting him no reproof, no probation, no
     rankling grudge;
   only forgiveness and the fullness of a father's love.

In whatever far country this day finds us,
   help us to come to ourselves, our own true selves,
   and so to come to thee.

Teach us to press our weakness close to thy strength
   that we may receive from thy fatherly hand
   the gifts of thy grace which are requisite for us all:
   pardon and cleansing for our sins, light for our darkness,
   courage for life's battle, endurance for life's pain.

We dare to ask this, not because we deserve forgiveness,
   but because it is thy nature to forgive,
   and because we ask in Jesus' name. Amen.

HE CAME TO HIMSELF

ONE EVENING years ago I was one of a group of students whose conversation turned to the question, "What is the greatest short story ever written?" The masterpieces of Guy de Maupassant, Robert Louis Stevenson, and Edgar Allen Poe were passed in review. Some one mentioned Edward Everett Hale's "The Man Without a Country." Another suggested the Book of Ruth. Another, Tolstoi's "Where Love Is There God Is Also." Another, Kipling's "The Drums of the Fore and Aft" and "The Man Who Would Be King." Dickens' "A Christmas Carol" received favorable consideration.

Finally the professor in whose hospitable study we were gathered said, "Let me read you what I consider the incomparable short story." Turning to the fifteenth chapter of Luke, he read the story of the Prodigal. It has well been called "the pearl of the parables." It is the one that comes closest to the heart of the gospel. Some think that with the two related parables of the Lost Sheep and the Lost Coin it is the longest piece of consecutive teaching we have from Jesus' lips.

A Disclosure of Jesus

It is first a disclosure of Jesus. One of life's thrills is to watch the touch of the master hand. It gives us pleasure to watch a display of skill—to watch a man operate a steam

145

shovel or a deft surgeon perform a delicate operation or a star outfielder field a ball and throw it home in one long, graceful motion.

Here is the master teacher. Before we listen to him, let us watch him. He is talking with tax collectors and sinners, with people who are no good; and—as the Pharisees are quick to point out—a man is known by the company he keeps.

As you read the gospels, watch for Jesus' eyes. There must have been something arresting in his glance. The only hint of his appearance I have been able to find is in three compounds of *blepein*, the Greek verb meaning "to look," which Mark uses to describe the look of Jesus: *emblepein*, "to look into," to look a thing straight in the face—the look of insight; *periblepein*, "to look around," to look at a thing on all sides— the look of comprehension; *anablepein*, "to look up," to lift up one's eyes—one of the New Testament verbs meaning "to pray."

Luke lets us see that Paul's characteristic gesture was to stretch out his hand before speaking, perhaps to quiet his audience. Jesus, it appears, looked men straight in the eyes, paused, then spoke. See how quickly he sizes up the situation. He hears the good people criticizing him for talking to these bad people. Without a hint of preparation, out come three perfect stories: the Lost Sheep, the Lost Coin, the Lost Son.

Can you tell a story? It is an art. Some try to tell a story and you have difficulty in finding the point, in knowing what they are driving at. There are passages in the New Testament that are hard to understand, as II Peter says of Paul's letters.

Anyone can understand the stories of Jesus, though the more we think about them the more we find in them.

It was said of the two great orators of antiquity that to Cicero you can add nothing and from Demosthenes you can take nothing away. The same might be said of the "Gettysburg Address" or the collects in *The Book of Common Prayer*. There is an inevitability in the diction. Not only is every word the right word but the construction of the sentences is right. The accent and emphasis fall in the right place. Form fits thought as hand fits glove or key fits lock.

Read these stories in the fifteenth chapter of Luke with this in mind. How would you change them? Can you add anything to improve them? Can you take anything away without spoiling them? This is what we mean by style. Even untutored folk who have never been taught to parse and analyze are aware of it. There is a fitness, a rightness, which they perceive, in which they take pleasure.

Some think that style is like lipstick—put on from the outside. True beauty comes from within. It is the emanation of "a spirit lucid, melodious, poised and whole." In the stories of Jesus the beauty comes from within. They are the overflow of a radiant personality.

Note how his characters come alive. There are no stereotypes, no lay figures. In the rich portrait gallery of Shakespeare there are many clowns but no two alike. Bottom the Weaver is different from Launcelot Gobbo. Touchstone is distinct from Feste. Neither blends into the most appealing of all, the Fool in Lear. There are two gravediggers in Hamlet. They appear in a single scene. But they are not just two gravediggers. Each is a personality in his own right. The same is true of even the minor characters created by the opulent imagination of Dickens. They are real people. If you prick them, they bleed.

So it is with the *dramatis personae* of Jesus. Some are touched off lightly, like the citizen of the far country to whom the prodigal in his extremity appeals. We can fill in the portrait for ourselves. The poor beggar knocks at his door, asks for a job. This philanthropist says to him, "Times are hard. A lot of people are out of work. You may go out in the fields and tend the pigs if you want to." The famished prodigal would have been glad to eat the pig food but "no one gave him anything."

Or the surly older brother. Do you note Jesus' irony when he speaks of the "ninety-nine righteous persons who need no repentance," as though any of us needs no repentance?

Or look at the shepherd. Dean Russell of Columbia tells of a shepherd he met on a walking trip through the Pyrenees. As he brought his flock back to the fold at night, he called each by a pet name. "How do you tell them apart?" asked the dean. "The same way you do people," said the shepherd, "by their faces." He had lived with them long enough and looked at them carefully enough to know each one.

This shepherd in the story goes over his sheep and discovers that one is missing. "I am going to search for it," he says. How long? an hour? two hours? five hours? "Until I find it." There is no thought in his mind of coming back without the sheep. He is that kind of man. Jesus likes that kind of man.

But Jesus omits one thing which a writer of fairy tales or the fake animal stories we read to children would have put in. He does not tell us what the sheep said when it was found. Why? Because the stories of Jesus are real.

Or look at the woman who has lost a coin. This thrifty soul has lost one of the precious coins she has been slowly accumulating, perhaps to pay her taxes, perhaps to buy something she needed for her home. To her the loss is a calamity. She says, "I am going to find that coin if I have to turn the house inside out and upside down." All told in a sentence, but we get the impression of energy, of determination. She is that sort of person. Jesus admires that sort of person.

Note that when the shepherd found the sheep and the woman found the coin, they did not say, "Well, that's that." Some of us want our friends to sympathize with us when we are in trouble. We forget to ask them to rejoice with us when good fortune comes our way. These people had to call in their neighbors and tell them about it. Jesus liked them for that.

A Disclosure of Ourselves

The story is not only a disclosure of Jesus but a disclosure of you and me.

One of the things we learn as we grow older is that people are seldom as uncomplicated as they appear. You look at them as they sit in church or on a bus or in a doctor's waiting room and wonder what goes on behind their stolid exteriors. You can tell little about a person from his casual conversation, from the face he shows the world. You put him down as a simple soul. His interior life may be far from simple. He looks like a healthy extrovert. His mind may be a labyrinth through which he himself cannot find the way, with dark corners where he dares not let in the light.

For some years I was minister of a downtown church in an eastern industrial city on the edge of a huge slum. Many of my people lived in tenements and hovels scarcely fit for human habitation. From there I was called to a church in one of the finest residential areas in America. My people lived in well-designed, well-appointed, tastefully furnished homes, with interior decorators to make sure the color schemes were right, landscape men to lay out the planting. Will you believe that in this favored group I found every kind of vice, perversion, appetite, maladjustment I had found in the Newark slums? As Kipling said, the colonel's lady and Judy O'Grady are sisters under the skin. If the secrets of our souls should be laid bare, who of us would not be filled with confusion and shame?

Edwin Arlington Robinson sings of Richard Cory:

> Whenever Richard Cory went down town,
> We people on the pavement looked at him:
> He was a gentleman from sole to crown,
> Clean favored, and imperially slim.
>
> And he was always quietly arrayed,
> And he was always human when he talked;
> But still he fluttered pulses when he said,
> "Good morning," and he glittered when he walked.

And he was rich—yes, richer than a king—
And admirably schooled in every grace:
In fine, we thought that he was everything
To make us wish that we were in his place.

So on we worked, and waited for the light,
And went without the meat, and cursed the bread;
And Richard Cory, one calm summer night,
Went home and put a bullet through his head.*

I do not imply that you and I are likely to do anything as desperate as that. I merely suggest that we are not quite as placid and unperturbed as we try to appear.

Jesus rarely called people sinners. He spoke of them as lost. A thing is lost when it is out of its rightful place and therefore failing to fulfill the purpose for which it was made. A coin is lost when it is out of circulation, no longer functioning as a medium of exchange. Men are lost not in the sense of being irreparably damned (these stories of the Lost Sheep, the Lost Coin, the Lost Son were told to correct such a hopeless creed) but in the sense of being off the course and so missing their destiny.

Some are lost like sheep, not from viciousness or conscious choice, but from heedlessness, not looking where they are going. Some are lost like coins, not through their own fault but through another's carelessness or life's mischance. Some are lost like the prodigal, through deliberate self-will. But all alike need to be found and restored.

Some years ago Stuart Chase wrote a book entitled *The*

* From Collected Poems of Edwin Arlington Robinson, Macmillan

Tragedy of Waste, to which he could add a few chapters were he to bring out a revised edition. The tragedy of the prodigal was a tragedy of waste. The squandering of his money was the smallest part of it. The waste of opportunity, of fine possibilities, of the hopes and dreams of youth: this is the saddest sight that earth affords.

It is not always due to sensuality. The journey need not end in a pigpen. In Winston Churchill's* novel, *The Far Country,* the hero's dissipation is not of bodily appetite. It is the dissipation of ideals that had once shone bright, the gradual lowering of standards in the practice of his profession. But Churchill shows how the tragedy is the same—the tragedy of waste, the waste of great gifts and high possibilities.

On the day the prodigal left home, his brother said to himself, "Good riddance." He would have looked on it as a blessing, a relief, if the boy had died. The purpose of the story is to show that this attitude is wrong. The shepherd sought the sheep because it had value. The woman sought the coin because it had value. Everyone said that the prodigal was a worthless scamp. But Jesus uses a remarkable expression concerning him: "when he came to himself." You would think that his self was the source of all his trouble. Jesus says no. His wayward impulses were not his real self. When he came to himself he said, "I am going back where I belong."

Note how this expression has entered into our language. When a friend has an irritable or ungenerous mood we say,

---

* Not the English statesman, but the American author of the same name.

"He is not himself." We know that irascibility is foreign to his true nature, which is genial and kind.

Jesus did not make light of sin. No one—not Aeschylus nor Shakespeare nor Ibsen nor Dostoevski nor Hawthorne nor Hardy—has traced its consequence with more stern fidelity than he. But he did not believe that sin is the final expression of human nature. He was sure that the deepest thing in man is fine. "When he came to himself"—such is the invincible optimism of Jesus. No one ever knew human nature as he did and no one ever put such a high value on man. He ends the story of the Lost Coin with an extraordinary statement: "There is joy before the angels of God over one sinner who repents."

In the thirty-eighth chapter of Job the poet depicts God as describing his creation, what Browning calls the beauty and the wonder and the shape of things, their colors, changes, surprises. He pictures God as viewing his creation as an artist might stand back to view a painting he has just finished and calling, "Have a look!" So they look and, says the writer, "the morning stars sang together and all the sons of God shouted for joy." That is sheer poetry, of course, but what a picture, what an imagination! Here is a more wondrous picture, a more daring imagination: joy in the eternal world over one man who, having sinned, resolves to sin no more.

Can you believe that? It is Jesus putting a higher value on you than anyone else has ever done, a higher value than you put on yourself. His faith in man is more amazing than his faith in God. No one ever took such risks with ordinary people. I mention two. He entrusted his cause and all it meant to the world to Peter, James, John and the rest of the little band. That is one. The other is that now he entrusts it to you and me, confident that we'll not let him down. He rates us higher than we dare to rate ourselves.

A Disclosure of God

The story of the Prodigal is a disclosure of Jesus; it is a disclosure of you and me; finally—and this brings us to the heart of it—it is a disclosure of God.

St. Augustine says that when in his day it was read in church the people wept. I told it once to a soldier whose life was ebbing away. When I came to the part where the prodigal, having wasted his substance in debauchery, sat down among the husks with the swine, he said, "Padré, you've been telling the story of my life." I said, "I've told you only half the story." Then I went on to tell how the father had never ceased to miss the boy, how he had watched for him all the time he was gone, looking down the road the first thing every morning, leaving a lamp in the window at night; how, as soon as the boy came to himself and started home, the father's love went out to meet him.

Aristotle says that the dignified man will never run. But this father does not stand on his dignity. While the boy is still a long way off, he sees him, recognizes him even in his rags, and runs down the road shouting, "Bring a robe, bring shoes, bring a ring, make a feast! For this my son was dead and is alive again; he was lost and is found."

That is a picture of God. Do you dare to believe that the infinite and eternal Spirit by whom the worlds were made is like that? A later prodigal, Aaron Burr, wrote to his daughter Theodosia, "I think God is a great deal better than people suppose." I think so, too. But do you believe that God feels for you as this father felt for his erring son?

I could not believe it apart from Jesus. It takes the cross to convince me of it. When I see him who told the story hanging with his arms stretched wide to gather every prodigal in, then I believe that

> ". . . the love of God is broader than the measure of
>   man's mind;
> And the heart of the eternal is most wonder-
>   fully kind."

"Where Are the Nine?"

A Song of Thanksgiving

God of all goodness and grace, prayer turns to song upon our lips as we thank thee for the benefits we receive from thy fatherly hand:

> for the good earth which nourishes our souls with beauty as it feeds our bodies with bread;

> for the day with its rich opportunities to work, to play, to learn, to serve;

> for night with its train of stars and its great gift of sleep;

> for the firm clasp of friendly hands, the ever lengthening web of association which binds us to our friends;

> for the bits of unselfishness with which we have brightened other lives and others have brightened ours;

> for words of encouragement we gave to those bearing heavy burdens and others gave to us:

> for hours of high communion with the seers and singers of mankind;

> for the sense of continuity which makes the present a bridge between a past of memories and a future of anticipation;

> for the love that arches all our years.

Impel us to show our gratitude in ways that will ensure to those who come after us as much of good as we have received from those who have gone before, that we too may help the sons of men on their toilsome pilgrimage toward the city of God. Amen.

"WHERE ARE THE NINE?"

THE INCIDENT we are about to study is found only in Luke (17:11-19).

Luke was a physician. He had a keen eye for the sick, a special interest in the cures which Jesus wrought and which he reports more fully than the other gospel writers.

There were ten lepers, ostracized from their fellow men by the loathsome disease which had befallen them.* These forlorn men had heard of Jesus' healing power. They met him as he was about to enter a certain village and, standing far off, cried, "Jesus, Master, have mercy on us." He answered, "Go show yourselves to the priests." In that old theocracy, the priests served as health officers. They quarantined cases of contagious disease and were empowered to issue certificates indicating that the quarantine was lifted. Jesus' reply was assurance that by the time they reached the priest they would be healed. "And it came to pass, as they went they were cleansed." One of the ten returned to Jesus and thanked him. "Were not ten cleansed?" asked Jesus, "where are the nine?"

One would suppose that men who had been relieved of so

---

* The book of Leviticus, which contains a good deal of health legislation, devotes the whole of its thirteenth chapter and part of its fourteenth to leprosy—the tests of leprosy, the behavior required of lepers. They were compelled to keep their distance, and if anyone approached to cry, "unclean, unclean." Eyes, ears and nostrils were offended by them; no one would touch them. Usually the disease progressed until their bodies literally fell to pieces.

grim a disease, restored to health and to the society of their families and friends and enabled to resume the activities of normal life would go far out of their way to show their appreciation. Such an assumption takes too rosy a view of human nature. The proportion of those who take the trouble to show that they are grateful for kindnesses received is exceedingly small. Sadly enough, to do a man a favor is often to lose his friendship. When he sees you, he is reminded that he is under obligation to you. He doesn't like to be reminded of it. So he shuns you.

For many years I have been trying to help people with money given to the church for benevolence or entrusted to me by generous individuals. I have had to cope with professional panhandlers, plausible rascals trying to solve the problem of living without work, "the undeserving poor," as Dickens called them: what the Christian attitude is toward this gentry I wish someone would tell me. Certainly they are not to be encouraged and they do not want to be reformed. I have helped worthy families with hospital expenses and funeral expenses, eye glasses and wheel chairs. I have helped young people with college expenses. I have had heart-warming experiences with people who have proved themselves pure gold; but all of you who have given your money, time and thought to helping people know that you could easily grow sour as you recall some of your experiences.*

---

* One of the Seven Sages of Greece—Chilon of Sparta, if my memory serves —said that the three most difficult things are to keep a secret, to forgive an injury and to make wise use of leisure. To these I add a fourth: to give money wisely, either one's own or the income of a charitable foundation.

"Where are the nine?" Lord, I'm astonished to hear you ask
that. You know human nature. If one out of ten comes back
to say "thank you," that is about the proportion to expect.

If you want to be a helper of men, you had better put your
helpfulness on some other basis than the expectation of gratitude. Otherwise, you let yourself in for disappointment If
they thank you, fine; if they don't, forget it. Try to be like
God who makes his sun shine and his rain fall on good and
evil, grateful and ungrateful, with impartial magnanimity.
Our conduct should never be determined by what other people do to us. We should be far more concerned with asking,
"Have I done the same to someone else?" I could get up a lot
more righteous indignation toward these ingrates were it not
for my disturbing memory.

Gratitude is not a conspicuous trait of youth. A young
person takes everything his parents and older friends do for
him as a matter of course and rarely feels it necessary to make
any return. Even if he says "thank you" because he's been
trained in politeness, it is with little appreciation of what the
kindness cost. I find it easy to forgive him, for all through
my boyhood and youth I did precisely the same. I have little
doubt that I was a nuisance to the relatives who were uni-
formly kind to me. I had uncles and aunts with summer
homes on the shore. Year after year they invited me to spend
my vacations with them. It was not till I was much older that
I realized it could not have been an unmitigated pleasure to
have an extra boy with a big appetite on their hands. I had a
high school teacher who took me to her home before I took the
College Board examinations and drilled me on the questions

which from her study of previous examinations she knew would be asked. I assumed I was doing her a favor by accepting her tutelage, that she was honored by having among her pupils a boy bright enough to take the College Boards. That's youth for you.

As we grow older we do not always grow in this grace. The more people do for us, the more we expect. The patient ministries of the home we accept as our due. Often we do not wake up until too late. When a minister is called into a home where a father, mother, husband, wife, brother, or sister has died, he often finds the survivors overcome with remorse, as they think of how much they have received and how little they have given. And I suspect (though this is not a nice thing to say) that many an expensive funeral, the casket covered with a costly blanket of roses that will be wilted before they reach the cemetery, is a belated attempt by a conscience-stabbed family to break the alabaster cruse of ointment whose fragrant contents should have been poured out long before.

"I Hate Ingratitude"

Although ingratitude is not one of the seven deadly sins of mediaeval theology, the moralists of the race have always regarded it as a major fault. Shakespeare speaks of it so feelingly as to indicate he had experienced it:

> Blow, blow, thou winter wind,
> Thou art not so unkind
>   As man's ingratitude . . .
> > Amiens, in *As You Like It*

This was the most unkindest cut of all;
For when the noble Caesar saw him stab,
Ingratitude, more strong than traitor's arms,
Quite vanquish'd him: then burst his mighty
    heart . . .
                Mark Antony, in *Julius Caesar*

How sharper than a serpent's tooth it is
To have a thankless child! . . .
                King Lear, in *King Lear*

I hate ingratitude more in a man,
Than lying, vainness, babbling, drunkenness,
Or any taint of vice . . .
                Viola, in *Twelfth Night*

It is interesting that Shakespeare ranks ingratitude with these gross derelictions, for it is a respectable sin, the sin of respectable people. Yet Dante, who was a specialist in sin, puts those guilty of disloyalty in the lowest circle of hell, and ingratitude is a form of disloyalty. It never stands alone. It is always accompanied by selfishness, often by hardness and pride.

Why are we, who admire loyalty and see how base ingratitude is, ever guilty of this sin? The question correctly assumes that most of us would have been among the nine lepers who went their way, that the same ratio prevails now as then. They were not necessarily villains. They may have been grateful in their hearts. They were naturally eager to get to their homes and families with the news of their good fortune. It did not occur to them that the only decent thing to do was to go back and say thank you. Their thanklessness was due to thoughtlessness. It is by no accident that in both English and German *think* and *thank, denken* and *danken,* come from the same root. Our ingratitude is the result of taking kindness as a matter of course. The most considerate of us can think of times when we have not been as thoughtful as we should have been to those who have been good to us. Some of them are dead. We cannot make it up to them now. We can make amends only by trying to do for someone else what they did for us. But it is likely that most of us can think of someone well along in years to whom we owe a kindness which in the pressure of our busy lives we have allowed ourselves to neglect.

This would be the most effective chapter I ever wrote if you and I should resolve in the secret place where decisions are made that from now on we will not take kindness for granted; if we should walk through the world with an almost tremulous sense that we have nothing we did not first receive. From the day we opened our baby eyes we have been recipients of a love we did not earn, a service we can never repay. We entered into a heritage bought by others' toil. The basic facilities of life, the things we use as carelessly as the pavement we tread—the fire we light; the alphabet we use; the decimal system; the wheels that carry us along; the internal combustion motor; the electricity that illuminates our homes, lightens our toil and carries our voices to those we love a thousand miles away—took character and ability. In many cases it took genius, the pooled genius of many men, each building on those who had gone before, to put these at our disposal.

There is not a blessing we enjoy, from our daily bread to our dear bought liberties and our Christian faith, that has not been won for us by the struggle and sacrifice of other men. He is indeed a shallow soul who can avail himself of them with never a thought of what they cost.

The Problem of Goodness

We carry the thought a step further when we think of it in relation to God. Thanksgiving Day is the one national holiday which has a religious origin and retains some semblance of religious character. Its central symbol is a feast, the Thanksgiving dinner. Far from regarding this as carnal, I think it a most meaningful symbol. It reminds us that every time we sit down to a meal, we eat a bit of God's creation. We appropriate it, assimilate it into our own bodies, which build it into the cellular architecture of muscle, flesh and blood. The strength, the fresh energy the food brings us is the gift of God. When we think of this, not only our Thanksgiving dinner, not only the bread and wine we pass amongst us in the beautiful rite known as the Eucharist, "the giving of thanks," but every meal becomes a sacrament, the outward and visible sign of an inner and spiritual grace.

When calamity befalls us we cannot help asking the question, "Why?" We are not nearly so ready to ask it concerning the goodness which befalls us. We talk about the problem of suffering, the problem of disease. And it is a problem. We can explain much on the ground of ignorance or abuse, but much remains unexplained. Why do we never speak of the problem of health? Most of us most of the time enjoy health: why do we take it for granted?

Our health is maintained and restored by the most ingenious arrangements which go on so unobtrusively we seldom think of them. When you cut your finger, your whole organism sets to work to repair the injury: the nervous system transmits the the signal of pain; the circulatory system pumps blood to the wound to wash it clean; the glandular system produces white corpuscles and rushes them to the spot to fight and expel in the form of pus the bacteria which would cause infection, making a wall of their tiny bodies to keep the bacteria from getting into the blood stream; finally, fresh blood comes up to form new tissue; and the wound heals. When a man contracts tuberculosis, part of the lung tissue is destroyed, but he has much more than he needs. He can call on his reserve and get along, as Dr. Trudeau did at Saranac for forty years, with only a part of one lung still functioning. Two fifths of the liver can be removed and the remaining three fifths will carry on the work of that organ as well as before. When a kidney is injured or infected, it is sometimes necessary to remove it. How does the surgeon dare to remove so vital an organ, with its many miles of tubes within which all sorts of processes go on? Because he knows that as soon as one kidney is removed, the other begins to grow until in a short time it is as big as the two were before and functions quite as well. When you see a surgeon in the course of an operation cut and tie thirty or forty blood vessels, you wonder what becomes of the blood that would otherwise circulate through them. The answer is that we have many more blood vessels than we need. We can be deprived of a good many and get on perfectly well with what are left. The normal body temperature is 98.6 degrees. A man can go into a temperature of twenty below zero or one hundred and twenty above zero, into a refrigerator or a boiler room, yet his temperature remains the same, such is the extraordinary capacity of the body to keep its balance in terms of heat. The brain does nothing about it. It is beyond our conscious power. It is part of the intelligent action of the body itself.

Think of the body's defenses. If a man is strained emotionally or physically beyond a certain point, nature says, "Take a rest," and he faints. When he comes to, he usually feels better. When a man takes poison into his system, the body endeavors to expel it. For example, it throws out alcohol through the lungs, which is why we smell it on the drinker's breath. I could give even more striking illustrations, but I do not want to become too clinical. I have given enough to indicate that a benign healing power fights on our side. Matthew Arnold defined God as the power outside ourselves that makes for righteousness. Here is a power inside ourselves that makes for health, that works day and night, when we are awake and when we are asleep, when we are good and when we are bad. This healing power is not neutral in the fight between us and the enemies of our health: it fights on our side and wins most of our battles for us. Here is one great reason for believing in the goodness of God, who through the long process of evolution built up our bodies to be the earthly dwelling of our souls.

Again, we speak of the problem of evil. It is the deepest and most baffling of all the problems of theology. If God is good and in control, why does he allow war? Why does he

allow evil men to wax strong and oppress their fellows? Why
does he allow the innocent to suffer? We can say with
reason that evil is a consequence of God's having endowed
man with a measure of freedom, that freedom to choose the
right must carry with it freedom to choose the wrong; God
had to take that risk. We can say with reason that many evils
which we blame on God have their explanation a long way
this side of God. Still much mystery remains. The more we
think about it the more of an enigma it becomes. But what I
want to ask now is, Why do we never speak of the problem
of goodness? All over the world, unseen and unrewarded,
men and women go on day after day, year after year, being
faithful, honest, kind and clean. They never get rich, they
never get fame, they have none of the incentives to virtue
that vulgar natures require, they just go on being good and
doing good until they die. How do you account for it?

We speak of the problem of pain, the problem of sorrow.
Why do we never speak of the problem of joy? Most of us
most of the time are happy; happy in our work, happy in our
play, happy in our relations with our fellow-beings. Most of
our normal activities have pleasurable overtones. We read a
good book, we hear a melody, we see a picture or a garden or
a sunset, we hold a baby in our arms or watch the unstudied
grace of a little child: the accompaniment of all these experiences is joy, joy which now and again becomes ecstasy. Is this
to be taken for granted? You say you don't deserve all the
evil that has come to you. Maybe not. Do you deserve all
the joy that has come to you? Or has it come as the free gift
of a God whose generosity goes far beyond what decency re-

quires, who gives because it is his nature to give good gifts to his children?

We speak of temptation, by which we mean temptation to wrongdoing. Why do we never speak of temptation to right-doing? A man I know had planned to put through a shady deal. He was on his way to do it when in the club car he met a younger man, the son of one of his friends. The younger man's obvious respect so affected him that he could not go through with what he had planned. When he reached his destination, he got on another train and went home. He told me the story—it seemed to him a divine interposition. All of us have had similar experiences, merciful escapes when our feet were close to the brink and something or someone interposed to save us. If there are incitements to evil, there are also guardian angels, loving presences, to save us from ourselves. All my life I have been surrounded by influences that have made me want to be better than I am. Why have I never before acknowledged it?

The Heart of Worship Is Praise

We have left the ten lepers a long way behind, but you see where our thought has been leading. One of the ten returned, glorifying God and giving thanks to Jesus. The heart of all worship is praise. Worship means literally "giving God his worth," and to give him his worth is to praise and adore. Most of our great hymns are hymns of praise; so are most of the psalms, the hymns of Israel. The question is sometimes asked, Why should we praise God? Is God like a vain woman or a conceited man who has to be continually flattered with praise in order to keep him in good humor? That misses the point. We praise him not chiefly for his sake (though it is conceivable he is not displeased by his children's appreciation), we praise him chiefly for our own. Praise is our response to a grace that is more than sufficient for us, a love that never fails. Whenever we think of them, we are "lost in wonder, love and praise." If the writer of the Revelation is correct, thanksgiving is the language of heaven. Unless we begin to learn that language here, we shall be dumb, inarticulate aliens there. Not only on Thanksgiving Day but every day we do well to repeat the exalted paean of praise we know as Psalm 103:

> Bless the Lord, O my soul,
> And forget not all his benefits:
> Bless the Lord, O my soul,
> And all that is within me, bless his holy name.

If I Be Lifted Up

Beneath the Covert of Thy Wing

Thou hast promised that, if with all our hearts we truly seek thee, we shall ever surely find thee. With all our hearts we seek thee now, O thou who art ever seeking us. To whom can we turn for fulfillment but to thee in whom our little lives are made complete? We reach past things we do not understand to clasp the hand of One who understands us. Silent as the coming of dawn, welcome as sunshine after many sunless days, pervasive as the air we breathe, strengthening as the food we eat be thy coming to us.

Hearten us to take each new day as a gift from thy hand, to live in it as they ought to live who know they are thy children, heirs of the eternal, fitted for communion with thee, with spirits as lasting as thine own, that, doing our duty, facing our temptations, bearing our griefs and burdens, we may prove ourselves Christ's steadfast soldiers and servants till the day's work is done and we lie down again to rest beneath the covert of thy wing. Amen.

IF I BE LIFTED UP

WHEN JESUS CHOSE to die on a cross, no one agreed with his choice. When he first broached the idea to his friends, they recoiled from it. Peter, their spokesman, said, "Far be it from you, Lord," to which Jesus answered, "Peter, you understand the ways of men but not the ways of God."

His enemies agreed with his choice, if choice they admitted it to be, only in the sense that it signified their triumph and his defeat. In the eyes of the populace of Jerusalem, it reduced his mission to a farce. A cross meant not a glorious martyr's death, it was merely a symbol of failure and of shame. It made no appeal to the popular imagination of the time. Even one hundred fifty years later Celsus, one of the keenest of the early opponents of the faith, taunted Christians because of "that great man of theirs who was stuck on a stick in Palestine."

Not everyone now agrees with Jesus' choice. There are those who—like the small boy who asked his mother for a Bible with nothing about the crucifixion in it—want a pleasant religion, a religion without tears. Bernard Show, an acute if unconventional amateur theologian, in the preface to *Androcles and the Lion* draws a distinction between Christianity and what he calls "Crossianity," animadverts on the church's preoccupation with the cross which seems to him morbid. H. G. Wells in God, the Invisible King declares that "the crucifixion, the drooping, pain-drenched figure of Christ . . . jar on our spirits." William Watson in a fine sonnet resents

> The Cross, the crown of thorns, the anguished eyes,
> The cruel wounds unstaunched and bleeding yet—
> Ever the same wan form before me set,
> All out of tune with the proud glorying skies!

and asks,

> . . . were it not more wise
> In his immortal greatness to forget
> The mortal agony and bloody sweat,
> And in his living words the dying cries?

Such men find the cross out of line with what William James calls "the religion of healthy mindedness," a healthy mindedness they are quick to ascribe to the life and teaching of the Man of Galilee.

There are others to whom the mass of doctrine which Christian thought centers in the cross is unintelligible or uncongenial or remote from everyday life. Hence the question, Why did Jesus deliberately plan his last journey to Jerusalem, seeing clearly what the outcome would be? is still a live one. For that he was not the helpless victim of circumstance but himself made the decision and forced the issue is conceded even by such radical critics of his life as Middleton Murray, English man of letters, and Claude Montefiore and

Abraham Klausner, Jewish students of Jesus, all of whom
delete from the gospel narrative every trace of the super-
natural as pious legend or later accretion, reducing Jesus to a
purely human, albeit heroic, figure. That Jesus chose the
cross is not in dispute. The question is, why?

Some of the greatest thinkers of Christendom—Augustine,
Anselm, Peter Abelard, John Calvin, Hugo Grotius, Friedrich
Schleiermacher, Albrecht Ritschl, Horace Bushnell—have
wrestled with the problem and set forth their successive
theories of the atonement, none of which is completely
satisfying. The "scapegoat theory" we recognize as a carry-
over from the Old Testament, a reading of Jewish sacri-
ficial ideas into the death of Jesus. The "ransom theory" we
see against the background of the feudal system which gave
it rise. Bushnell's "moral influence theory" is good as far as
it goes, but we can't help thinking that there is more in the
cross than moral influence.

Before the theologians had formulated their answers, Jesus
himself had given an answer. Here it is: "I, when I am lifted
up from the earth, will draw all men to me." Moreover, before his still warm body was taken down from the cross, the
experience of humanity had begun to make good his claim—
three men had been drawn to him by the cross. Let us look
at them in turn.

A Penitent Thief

The first was a penitent thief who said to Jesus, "Remember
me when you come to your kingdom"; to whom Jesus replied,
"Today you will be with me in Paradise."

It was, then, a sinful man paying the just penalty for his

deeds who was first to be drawn to Jesus when he was lifted up. This is significant. It means that the cross has something to do with sin.

Sin is not a popular subject in our enlightened time. We hear it said that modern man has lost the sense of sin. Those who say so imply that it is small loss. "Cultivated people," said Sir Oliver Lodge, "no longer worry about their sins." Maybe his observation is correct.

One reason Jesus chose the cross was sin. We may explain this as we will. Perhaps if a group of Christians were appealed to one by one, no two explanations would agree. But the experience of humanity through the centuries proclaims that the death of Jesus on the cross somehow has to do with sin. A score of hymns might be cited. Here is one:

> There is a green hill far away
>   Outside a city wall
> Where the dear Lord was crucified
>   Who died to save us all.
>
> There was no other good enough
>   To pay the price of sin;
> He only could unlock the gate
>   Of heaven and let us in.

You don't know what that means? Nor do I. But thousands who have felt their sin an encumbrance, an impediment, have been drawn to Jesus because they believed that his cross had some bearing on their sin.

Our fathers regaled themselves with Jules Verne's highly imaginative fantasies, the original science fiction. Modern inventiveness has made some of them passé. *Twenty Thou-*

sand Leagues under the Sea does not sound too exciting when nuclear powered submarines can cross the ocean without surfacing. Nor does *Around the World in Eighty Days* when jet planes can circle it in hours. But the one of which I am thinking now, though published in 1865, has a contemporary sound, *A Journey from the Earth to the Moon.*

In the course of the journey the men in the spaceship threw a dead dog from a window. They supposed it would fall away from them. They forgot they were beyond the pull of the earth's gravitation. There was no other object to attract the dead dog, no power inside the ship strong enough to expel it. So it clung outside the ship, formed a satellite to the ship. As they journeyed on, it went with them. They could not get rid of the loathsome thing. Finally it began to prey on their minds like the albatross in *The Rime of the Ancient Mariner.*

This is how many feel about sin. There is no power in ourselves strong enough to throw off the unclean, loathsome things that cling to us. The sense of moral failure, remorse for irreparable damage done to others, the memory of cruel words spoken to one long dead, foul imaginings which fill us with disgust but from which we cannot shake ourselves free: these cause sensitive souls to long for something or someone to wash them clean, to ask, as Macbeth asked his physician,

> Canst thou not minister to a mind diseased,
> Pluck from the memory a rooted sorrow . . .
> And with some sweet oblivious antidote
> Cleanse the stuff'd bosom of that perilous stuff
> Which weighs upon the heart?

Thousands have been convinced that, though we cannot understand the rationale of forgiveness, Jesus was speaking not poetry but fact when he said at the Last Supper, "This cup is the new covenant in my blood which is poured out for many for the remission of sins."

John Bunyan begins his allegory by picturing "a man clothed with rags with his face from his own house, a book in his hand and a great burden upon his back," who as he watched him "brake out with a lamentable cry saying, 'What shall I do? I am undone by reason of a burden that lieth hard upon me. I care not what I meet if so I can also meet deliverance from this burden.'" It was only when he came in sight of the cross that his burden loosed from off his back and fell and rolled into an open sepulchre and he saw it no more; stood there a long time, weeping, laughing, wondering. For it seemed strange that the sight of a cross could free him from the burden of his sin. Yet so it was. And in that Bunyan was writing the spiritual biography of multitudes beside his own.

It is not surprising that a man conscious of his sin first learned the truth of Jesus' words, "I, when I am lifted up from the earth, will draw men to me."

A Roman Soldier

The second was a different type: a Roman soldier, the officer in charge of the squad assigned the disagreeable business of executing the three condemned men.

He had no sins to confess—at least none that he was con-

scious of or wanted to confess. An honest man, loyal and
trustworthy by the standard of the army in which he served.
He had little understanding of what Jesus' offense was or why
they wanted him hung. These Jews, these religious fanatics—
past a plain man's comprehension. Do your duty, get on with
your job: that was his religion, all the creed he knew.

He watched Jesus die. He had seen men die before, seen
them die this same horrible death. A soldier becomes calloused
to the sight of suffering, he does not sentimentalize about it.
But he had never seen anyone die as this man died, comfort-
ing a dying thief in the midst of his own agony, breathing a
prayer of forgiveness for those who had nailed him there,
saying at the last, "It is finished," in a tone which declared
him victor rather than victim. As he watched through the
long hours, a conviction slowly took form in this soldier's
mind. He expressed it in his own blunt way: "Truly this man
was a son of God."* Saying which, he was second to record
that he was drawn to Jesus by the cross.

He also represents a type, a type which knows why Jesus
chose the cross with a directness and a certainty more subtle
folk miss. Plain men, matter-of-fact men who know nothing
of the mystic's rapture or the prophet's ecstasy, they none-
theless know one reason why Jesus chose the cross. He chose
it because it chose him, because in no other way could he
finish what he had set out to do. It was there as part of his
duty. Loyalty to his duty compelled him to accept it.

Why it had to be so is beyond a simple soul's ability to ex-

---

* According to Mark, followed by Matthew. Luke reads, "Certainly this
man was innocent!"

plain. It is beyond his ability to explain many of the hard things which have to be gone through if his own duty is to be done, his task in life fulfilled. It remains that Jesus chose the cross because it was part of his job. So it is that he, being lifted up, draws honest, faithful men to him. Doing his duty, he rallies them to do theirs.

A Leading Citizen

The third man represents the type to which many of us belong. This was Nicodemus "who at first came to Jesus by night," attracted to him, but not wanting to jeopardize his own standing by avowing it openly, and so came under cover of darkness. He was a Pharisee, a ruler of the Jews, a member of the Sanhedrin, the supreme court of Palestine, a man of light and leading, culture and refinement—modest, courteous, grave.

He represents the privileged class. He had been reared in the ways of conventional religion. He had some aptitude for spiritual understanding. He had known Jesus for some time. Jesus had said things to him of deep spiritual import such as he seldom spoke to any outside the intimate circle of his friends. It is in connection with Nicodemus' interview with Jesus that the words occur which have sung their way down the centuries and are often called "the gospel within the gospel": "For God so loved the world that he gave his only Son, that whoever believes in him should not perish but have eternal life. For God did not send his Son into the world to condemn the world but that through him the world might be saved."*

Nicodemus had not seemed to grasp it. At least he had not responded, left all to follow Jesus, throwing in his lot with the less sophisticated men who made up Jesus' little band. Think what it would have meant to Jesus to have had a man of Nicodemus' trained intelligence in his company. To be sure Nicodemus had more at stake than these humbly circumstanced men, more to lose than a fisherman like Peter, or a tax collector like Matthew. He had prestige and position.

Some have thought that his attitude was like that of the rich young ruler who also was attracted to Jesus but who turned away when Jesus told him plainly what discipleship entailed; that Nicodemus lacked the courage of his convictions, the resolution to follow through.

I wonder if Nicodemus was not rather the type to which many of us belong, those to whom religion is a strong cultural interest which appeals to our aesthetic and altruistic impulses; who want to give religion a place in our own and our children's all around development; who have an amiable desire that the cause of Christ succeed; but to whom religion has never become a passion and a transforming power, demanding all we have and all we are.

When Nicodemus saw Jesus lifted up, he broke through the shell of his staid, conventional, safe and sane religion. He had

* One of the problems of the Fourth Gospel is to disentangle the actual words of Jesus from the writer's reflections upon them and upon him. Did Jesus speak the hallowed words found in John 3:16-17, or did the writer say them about him? In either case they grew out of his conversation with Nicodemus.

already defended Jesus in the Sanhedrin, the only one who voted against his condemnation. He and Joseph of Arimathea (at what risk to themselves!) took Jesus' body down from the cross, prepared it for burial and carried it to Joseph's tomb. Then he perceived how God loved the world.

The Types Persist

So the first Good Friday called to the stage of history three men, each of a different type. The types persist.

There are the out and out rascals, the black sheep, for whom the world has no use but to put them out of the world, as with the thief on the cross. Christ had hope for him. "Today you will be with me in Paradise," he said to him and to all like him whose repentance is sincere.

There are the plain men, the rough diamonds, like the Roman soldier, who make little pretense to spirituality, whose religion is summed up in the dogged doing of their duty. Christ has the ways of God to reveal to them by his cross.

There are the good people, intelligent, well-disposed, responsible people, the salt of the communities in which they live, who have their standards, who try to live uprightly and not to do deliberate wrong. But they need the cross to point them to the heart of God.

Somewhere among these types we come. For all three types Christ makes his astounding claim, "I, when I am lifted up from the earth, will draw all men to me."

He had hardly breathed his last before his words began to prove true.

Will You Also Go Away?

At the Transit of the Years

O Thou who hast been man's dwelling place in all
    generations,
Who hast mercifully and patiently brought us to the
    gateway of another year,
Before we cross its threshold we confide our lives once
    more to thy holy keeping.

As we come to the successive stages of life
Help us to perceive that we do not face them alone;
That around our puzzled minds is the wisdom of the
    Most High,
Around our tired hearts is thine unwearied strength,
Around our need the love of One who sees the end from
    the beginning.

We know not what the future holds
But we know who holds the future.
We know not what the new year may bring;
We know it can bring with it nothing but thou wilt
    bear us through.

So may we set out upon it
With high heart and confident expectancy,
Sure that thou who hast brought us so far on our way,
Whose goodness and mercy have followed us all our days,
Hast new and richer splendors to disclose to us in the
    years to be. Amen.

WILL YOU ALSO GO AWAY?

Toward the end of the sixth chapter of John we read, "From that time many of his disciples drew back and walked no more with him." John indicates that there was a definite moment when Jesus ceased to be attractive or convenient for many. He saw them slip away, the thousands dwindle to hundreds, the hundreds to scores, till only a handful were left. That is a bitter pill for a man to swallow. It is likely to make him lose confidence in himself and in human nature, fickle, wavering, irresolute human nature.

To be sure, the Twelve stood their ground. Whether Jesus saw in their faces something which suggested even they might leave him, we cannot say. We know only that he looked at them—with what tenderness, what wistful pleading, who can tell?—and asked, "Will you also go away?"

This happened, John tells us, at a definite moment in Jesus' ministry. It was "from that time." From what time? From the moment when he hinted to them that to follow him further meant to follow to a cross. "From that time many drew back and walked no more with him."

A Day When We Have to Decide

Life is always leading us to a point where our dominant principles are put to the test. We may go for days without anything happening which forces the issue between duty and inclination, between one way of life and another. We may meet only good people with whom it is easy and pleasant to live on a high level, who, far from pulling us down, help hold us up to the mark we have set.

But soon or late a day arrives when we see what our principles involve and to what they lead us, when we have to decide whether to follow them into danger and sacrifice or abandon them. There is no clearer sign of God's presence in the world judging men than that days come when we may accept a cross in allegiance to the highest or turn our backs on it to protect our comfort and ease. There is no surer sign that this earth is, as John Keats called it, "a vale of soul-making" than that days come when we may accept a cross or reject it. Such a day had come to those who were following Jesus.

A Crisis Separates the False from the True

"From that time many drew back and walked no more with him." The commentators speak of this as "the crisis in Galilee." In our school days we learned to chart the plot of Shakespeare's tragedies: rising action to climax, falling action to catastrophe.

This was the crisis of Jesus' career. Till now his star had been in the ascendant. The Galileans had flocked to his movement and given it an air of success. The common people heard him gladly. He had taught them and healed them. Mark, describing a typical day in Capernaum, asserts that all the city was gathered at his door. To this point his ministry had been one of growing influence and power. From this point the downward action begins. From now on his way leads toward a cross.

The primary meaning of the Greek word *krinein* is "to separate"; the derived meaning, to separate good from bad, to judge. A day of crisis is a day of judgment, when men are tried and found adequate, or tried and found wanting. Such a day had arrived for the casual followers of Jesus, a day such as comes to us all and finds out whether the faith and loyalty we profess are real or sham.

They had been following Jesus without thinking much about what they were doing. They had seen others following and had joined the crowd. They had friendly feelings toward him, an amiable wish that his cause might prosper. He had spoken to them words of truth and grace. So far all had been sunny and bright. Suddenly the weather changed. The sky grew dark. Storm clouds gathered ominously on the horizon. At the first warning drops of rain, they scurried for cover, perhaps angry with themselves for having been taken in.

You can never depend on crowd enthusiasm, never tell from one day to the next what a crowd will do. A crowd is not a thinking body, it is a mixture of animal magnetism and unreason. A demagog, a hypnotist can do with it as he pleases. Jesus had the crowd and, not being a demagog or hypnotist, could not hold it. He looked on sadly while it melted away. This was his rejection in Galilee. His own district had turned him down.

Why did these false disciples draw back and walk no more with him? Because he spoke to them of the cross, which he now clearly foresaw. Had they stayed, he would have told them more and maybe their hearts would have been touched and their wills stiffened. He would have told them that when men are not daunted by the cross, when they share what Franz Liszt called its madness and elevation, they find there is more in it than pain—there is communion with God, the deep peace of resting in the everlasting arms.

He had no chance to tell them, for they had gone. The cross had scared them. They were willing to be hangers-on in his company without meaning much and without wanting him to infer they did mean much. When he told them plainly that any contact with him, however lightly begun, must either go on to become more and more or be broken, they drew back and walked no more with him.

The Final Pang

As he watched these fickle folk disappear, muttering their disappointment and disgust, he turned to the Twelve and asked if they too would leave him. Perhaps they were debating the question in their own minds, self-preservation pulling in one direction, loyalty in the other. It is not easy to stand fast when those around us are giving way. Mob psychology is a potent force. Few are strong enough to resist it. Maybe the Twelve too were dismayed by what Jesus saw ahead for himself and for them. "No," you say, "for did not Peter reply, 'Lord, to whom shall we go? You have the words of eternal life and we have believed and know.'"

This does not convince me that Peter did not for a moment hesitate. Do you not know what it is to catch yourself on the edge of an abyss, realize with a shudder where you are and spring back with all the strength you can muster? That vehement protest, far from proving we were not tempted, proves that for a moment we were.

Whether the Twelve had for a moment caught the infection of disloyalty we need not inquire. For, thank God, we are in the hands not of one who takes delight in showing up our momentary disloyalties but of one who judges us in the light of all we are and strive to be and of his own great pity and forgiveness. We only know that Jesus asked, "Will you also go away?"

To be left in the lurch by those who know nothing about him may cause a good man a pang. When people do not respond to his overtures of friendship, a good man asks in humility, "What's wrong with me?" To be deserted by those who have accepted our help is a bitter experience. To be forsaken by those to whom we have confessed our need of them, our loneliness without them: this is the final pang.

Something of this must have been in Jesus' soul when at this crisis in his career he appeals to the Twelve: "All these have left me. Why not? They do not know me. But you know me. You know how much I need you. Will you also go away?"

His Last Appeal

Can it be he looks at us with the same wistful pleading and asks, "Will you also go away?" For many who once followed him now walk with him no more.

In every city and town are men and women born of Christian parents, reared in Christian homes, trained in Christian truths by Christian pastors and Sunday school teachers, many of them graduates of colleges founded and maintained by the gifts of Christian people, beneficiaries of a Christian civilization (insofar as our civilization is Christian), living on inherited moral capital, who have gone off and left the whole thing. The church—as we have noted before—does not confront active hostility today except in lands where the religious situation is involved in the political situation: in China and the lands behind the Iron Curtain. But it is handicapped, its power diminished, its service curtailed, by the chilling indifference of those whom it has a right to expect to be its loyal friends.

Sometimes they say they had too much of it when they were young, a mean animadversion on their parents who were trying to pass on something they themselves had found good and hoped and believed would help their children. Or they explain that the pressure of their work is so great they have to sleep on Sunday, though most of them work a five-day week, have all Saturday to rest and play.

I do not mean to be hard on them. They are not bad people, just heedless, frivolous, worldly people, too shallow to perceive that to whom much is given, of them is much required. They'd do you a good turn if they could, and that's something. But when it comes to setting forward Christ's cause, they count for nothing. Indeed, no indifference, no unbelief is so stubborn as theirs. The same amount of effort on the foreign field will produce five times as many converts as from among these baptized pagans here at home.

But now the Lord Jesus looks at us who still walk with him and asks, "Will you also go away?" However little we want to make of it, there is a difference between the church and the world. It was not to the world Christ entrusted his cause. It was to those who know and love him, to whom he has shown his need of them, his dependence on them.

It was not for the world he prepared the supper the night before he died. It was for those on whom he counted to carry on his work in the world and for the world when he was gone. When he gave them those deathless symbols of the broken body and the shed blood, it was his last appeal that when he died, they should not let him die.

It is a sobering thought that in the prayer he offered there in the upper room, he prayed for you and me: "I pray not for the world but for those whom thou hast given me . . . nor for them only but for those who are to believe in me through their word . . . Father, I desire that they also may be with me where I am."

I think I see the print of nail-pierced feet in the path where we must go. But when his question comes to us, "Will you also go away?" may we answer quick and clear:

O Jesus, I have promised to serve thee to the end;
O give me grace to follow, my master and my friend.

A Prayer

O Christ, who didst bid thy disciples, "Learn of me";
    who taught them to ask, expecting to receive;
    to seek, expecting to find;
    to knock, expecting closed doors to open;
    make us willing to keep on being educated by thee
    until our minds are informed and illumined by thine.
Then help us to become more like thee,
    to expect more from thee,
    to do more for thee,
    to let thee do more for us. Amen.

Ascription

To thee, God the Father, by whose power we were
    created and by whose love we are redeemed;
To thee, God the Son, in whom the word became flesh
    and dwelt among us;
To thee, God the Spirit, our strengthener and guide,
    be glory forever. Amen.